Minutes Not Money

Minutes Not Money by Todd Cook

Copyright © 2018 by Todd Cook
All rights reserved, including the right to reproduce any portions of this book in any form.

Table of contents

Minutes Not Money 4

Generations of Wealth 20

What do you truly love 29

90 VS 10 31

True Wealth is Time 39

The Magic Trick of Making Money 42

A Different Way to Think 44

Breaking Away From the Crowd 51

Mistakes and Failures 63

The 9 of Hearts 73

P + R = O 76

Land of The Free 82

The Value of Life 91

Industrial Age vs Information Age	92
Risky Business	100
Destroying The Myths of Debt	134
The Success Pyramid	170
Master of Time	175
Master of Money	179
Finding Startup Money	192
Summary	194
Acknowledgements	197

Minutes Not Money
You can't win the game if you don't know the rules

    I can't remember how many times I've been told I'm obsessed with money, or been accused of thinking about money instead of the important things in life. I don't deny it, I do think a lot about money but for reasons far different than what I'm accused of. It isn't for the spacious mansion in Beverly Hills or the flashy Maserati - not saying I wouldn't buy either one - but that's not why I pursue knowledge of money.

    I'm going to be very upfront and open with you, I have enjoyed a very successful career as a pilot which has allowed me the time and money to attempt and fail at many different business ventures. I have been blessed with very good health and a clear mind making all of this possible. I have learned a great deal about money over the last twenty years and I still have a very long way to go. Only in recent years have I discovered the meaning of true wealth and passive income. I have some very influential friends and I've been introduced to some incredibly successful people whom I continue to learn from every day. I'm inviting you to join me on my personal journey to financial independence and hopefully we can get there together.

What I'm going to share with you is based on what I have experienced and continue to experience in my personal life. Everything I will share is a combination of the books I've read, the lessons I've learned from my many personal failures, as well as what I did right on a few occasions. I will share what I learned while spending thousands of dollars on coaches and mentors hopefully saving you a few bucks in the process.

It took me the better part of forty years to discover that true wealth is time. You are never truly free or truly wealthy unless you can do what you want, when you want with the minutes of your life.

I am going to share with you what I wish someone would have told me twenty years ago. I will do everything possible to provide you with true and accurate information. Keep in mind, I continue to learn new things every day. Some of what I know today could have changed or could possibly be wrong. What I'm saying is, don't take my word for it but put the information to the test and customize it to fit your own life and beliefs.

This book contains information I have shared over the years in my live seminars, as well as information from my top ranking podcast, Minutes Not Money. The podcast was ranked #4 in the Itunes new and noteworthy section, investing category.

When my oldest daughter turned eighteen and moved away to college, I realized I had missed everything. My career as a pilot cost me life's most precious minutes that no amount of money could replace. I have missed ball games, birthdays, school plays, even holidays, I even missed the birth of my youngest daughter Jessica. I was in Great Falls, Montana when I got the call from my wife in Utah telling me she was going into labor.

"Good luck" was all I could say.

I guess all of this would have been ok if it were for a valiant cause like the brave men and women serving in the military, and my heart goes out to them, but mine was for a job.

The realization that my dream of becoming a pilot had cost me the minutes most valuable to me was the birth of my "*WHY*" for writing this book. Quite literally my dream job as a commercial pilot had become my life's biggest regret. My dream had turned into a nightmare. If I can help you miss one less school play or one less ball game, or even a birthday then I will consider this book a success.

All my ancestors that have passed on, spent a lifetime gaining knowledge and wisdom about people, life, and money. But they never left any of that wisdom behind other than in words they may have spoken to others over the years. What they said to others was of little use to me.

How amazing would it be to have a book written by them teaching us everything they had learned? It would allow us to pick up where they left off. Instead, we have to start from scratch just like they did over 80 years ago, only to die after we finally figure out what they already knew. If I never sell one copy of this book it won't matter. I'm simply leaving behind what I know about money at this point in my life. Is it right or wrong? I don't know. Only time will tell. Take what you like and disregard the rest. As fast as things are changing it's quite possible that none of it is accurate anymore. But I'll give you what I know and leave it up to you.

If you take nothing else away from this book, remember this, true wealth is time. Time is all that matters, you can never make more of it, the last 60 seconds are gone forever.

Buckminster Fuller defined true wealth as:
"The number of days you can go and maintain your current lifestyle without you or anyone in your family physically working for money."

In other words, if you lost your job today, how many days could you go before you are forced to change your current lifestyle? Like downsizing your home or selling your car for something more affordable. The average household could last about 14 days. True wealth is time. How much of your time is yours to do what you want when you want to do it?

My purpose is to use my determination and confidence to free the masses from the prison that was created for their minds, to uplift and inspire others to go for their dreams, work together, and enjoy life with no financial concerns.

I have spent the last twenty years in the study and observation of the differences between people with money and those without. I discovered that becoming a master of your time and your money is a must, no matter how large or small the amount.

I will share with you everything I have learned and continue to learn about time and money, including the truths and myths about it. I will provide you with valuable tools and insights, designed to help you turn your money into minutes.

WHY

I grew up in a very economically depressed area. Even today if you make $35,000 a year, you're in the top 10% income bracket in my hometown. The area barely survives off of it's agricultural background and it's smelly turkey farms, yes, the very turkeys whose destiny is to end up on a dining room table for Thanksgiving.

As a young boy living on a farm, we had a beautiful red brick home my father had built. He is an excellent carpenter and had a shop located about two miles away in town. At that point, life was good, I even had my own horse named Hance, he was a tall brown, quarter horse and was great with kids.

Shortly after I turned twelve, the seventh sibling in the family, my youngest brother was born. He decided he wanted to enter the world two months earlier than his due date. Unlike today, in the early 1980's this was a big deal and cause for great concern. Unfortunately, along with other complications both my brother and mother spent the next two months in the hospital. Needless to say, the medical bills were more than my family could handle and we lost everything and I mean everything. In came the bank, repossessing the farm, my father's cabinet shop, our wonderful home, and yes, they even took my horse.

From that day on, the backpack I carried to school was not one of books. It was much heavier than that, it was the backpack of financial insecurity. Little did I know I would carry that backpack for the better part of 30 years.

I heard a quote the other day that made me laugh, "I've been poor and I've been rich. Rich is better."

Since the day we lost the farm, anytime I heard someone say "money can't buy happiness" I wanted to kick them in the teeth.

"*Have you ever been without*?" I would think to myself.

I have seen the look of hunger on my children's faces. There was a desperate point where we had to dig through the couch cushions, looking for enough change to buy a box of macaroni and cheese for dinner one night. Only a parent down on their luck at a point such as this, could understand the mental burden this places on a person. I was the second generation in this scenario, going through the same thing my father went through when I was twelve.

My father took a part-time job as a truck driver to help pay the bills. He was gone on a two week run when my mother and I loaded our washer and dryer into our pickup truck. Keep in mind I was twelve at the time. We were headed for town where we moved our family of nine into a small, two bedroom rental home. The bank later repossessed the truck as well.

Over the years, I've never forgotten the feeling I had as a twelve-year old boy during the first Christmas we spent in that small, two bedroom rental home. The look of stress on my father's face is still so prominent in my mind, seven kids, $125 to his name, and rent was due.

It's true you can't buy a gallon of happiness from your local grocery store, but try going without and see just how happy you are.

A few years later, the old abandoned schoolhouse in town went up for auction. Everyone else saw a worthless old building, but my father saw a new home for his family. At $14,000 he was the highest bidder and we soon moved into the place I still call home to this day. My father put his cabinetry skills to work and over the next several years turned that old building into a large, beautiful and comfortable home.

Since turkeys were the main source of income in my town, many farmers chose to raise their turkeys in long metal barns "turkey barns" are what we call them. Having lost the farm, I found employment with other farmers in the area. One of them had a turkey barn with a lean-to attached to the side of it. The lean-to ran the length of the barn, it was roughly 100 feet long and 20 feet wide.

Picture if you will, two or three thousand turkeys living inside this lean-to for the better part of twenty weeks, not one of them potty trained. This resulted in a two foot thick layer of turkey waste saturated sawdust covering the entire floor of the lean-to. Yes, it smells as bad as it sounds. Unfortunately for me, the door on the lean-to was not large enough to fit a tractor through it. My unlucky job, was to fill a wheelbarrow with this rotten mixture of manure and sawdust using nothing but a shovel and pitchfork. I would then push the wheelbarrow the length of the lean-to up a narrow wooden plank and over a two foot high cement wall that formed the base of the door leading outside. After what felt like eternity but in reality was only a few days, the lean-to would be clean and ready for the next group of turkeys to start the same unsanitary cycle all over again. What was left outside was a very large pile of turkey manure, which was then hauled to the fields and used as fertilizer.

I found a treasure at the bottom of that pile of manure, I discovered an unbelievably strong desire and determination to find a better way to make a living.

I always knew I wanted to fly but never believed it possible. I mean, honestly, a small town boy from the middle of nowhere wanting to be a commercial pilot? Yeah, right! Even if I thought I had what it takes to be a pilot, I would never be able to afford the mandatory training for the job. I thought it was an unrealistic goal for a young boy whose family had just lost their home and had just enough money to put food on the table. Life would soon teach me that where there's a will, there's a way, and how I became a captain for a commercial airline is a story I will save for another time and place.

As a pilot, I have stayed in five star all inclusive resorts, played on the sunny beaches of Monterey Bay, been to the Master Golf Tournament in Augusta, Georgia. Not to mention trips all around the world to places like Denmark, Germany, and England. I have had the incredible opportunity to visit just about every major city in North and South America.

I have flown over thirty different types of aircraft. Starting from small homebuilt airplanes to private jets for famous football players and movie stars. Also including my personal favorite aircraft, a World War II trainer for fighter pilots called a BT-13. I have done just about everything you can do in an aircraft including all the thrilling upside down aerobatics. I even became a skydiving coach and started jumping out of them.

I have literally spent more hours in the sky than I have on the ground in a car. All of this thanks to two things, desire and determination, that I found at the bottom of a pile of turkey manure.

In 1999 while flying private jets, I was making more money than any other time in my life. But something was wrong, I noticed my financial backpack was still there and was now heavier than ever.

After an unfortunate dip in the stock market, my employer sold the learjet I was flying and I soon found myself unemployed. Once again we lost everything except, my financial backpack.

Much to my disappointment I discovered that everything I thought I knew about money was wrong. I thought if I made a lot of money, my financial concerns would go away. Ha, yeah right!

Six months later, I found a job with an airline out of Washington D.C, life was once again good, although the heavy financial backpack was still there.

September 11, 2001 a group of terrorists crashed hijacked aircraft into the World Trade Center in New York. They also crashed one into the Pentagon that was located directly under the normal flight path for aircraft landing at Reagan National in Washington D.C. I had flown that very flight path many times myself. This event became sorrowfully known as 9/11.

The airline I was working for happened to be based in Washington D.C, and was shut down completely. I was yet again unemployed and we lost everything, except for, you guessed it, the financial backpack. I learned it didn't matter how much money I did or didn't have, the backpack always remained.

Left with no choice, I used the last of my free flight benefits and put my incredibly supportive wife, along with our four small children on an airplane headed for home to move in with the in-laws.

We had less than $50 in our bank account and I didn't have a clue as to how I was going to get myself and the few possessions we had left back home. A few days later my father made the 2000 mile journey one way to help me load what little we had left into a small car, along with a rented U-Haul. My brother in-law had called and offered to pay for the U-Haul rental and my uncle, a turkey farmer, had sent a letter with my father.

In it was a note that said,

"I don't know why, but I had a strong feeling you would be needing this. I hope all is well."

Enclosed was a check for $1,000 more than enough to cover the cost of fuel and food for the 2000 mile trip home. I couldn't hold back the tears as I stared at the letter, my uncle had no way of knowing that I was completely out of money or how badly I needed money at that very moment. Feeling discouraged but recharged, we started the 2000 mile trip across the country, right back to where I had started, turkey country.

Once again I found myself unable to hold back the emotions as I saw the city limit sign of my hometown. Everything I had done in my life was to help me get out of that economically depressed town. It was without a doubt the most discouraging day of my life, I was right back where I had started.

Don't get me wrong, my home town is full of wonderful people, the kind you can't find anywhere else. They are truly a genuine and kind-hearted group of people. Truth be told, part of why I decided to move home was because I knew the good farmers of that area would give this old boy a job.

Within a few short weeks I found myself standing directly inside that very lean-to I had worked in fifteen years earlier. Not one thing had changed, the smell, the look, even the shovel was exactly the same. It was as if time had stood still. I fought major discouragement with every shovel full.

Exhausted from shoveling I thought to myself, *"How does one go from flying multi-million dollar aircraft, back to shoveling turkey manure?"*

I must have asked myself that question hundreds of times a day, after all, the job didn't require much brain power and it left me with plenty of time to think. I use the word manure because I know my kids will be reading this, but it's far from the actual word I was thinking. Was this my fate? Was this my destiny? Am I destined to shovel turkey manure for the rest of my life? Lucky for me, my old friend's, desire and determination, still lived inside that barn.

Once again I was determined to find a better way to make money and my *"WHY"* grew stronger every day.

Fortunately, with several part time jobs from various farmers and a small handyman business I had started, we managed to keep our kids from starving to death.

A little over a year later, I once again returned to flying for a regional airline out of Salt Lake City, Utah. It took the next six years to recover financially and for my wife and I to feel like we could finally breathe after suffocating economically for so many years.

In the year 2007 I was now making ten times the amount of money my wife and I had made our first year of marriage combining both our incomes together. Keep in mind we were both in college and only working part time that first year. Life should have been great in 2007, and it was, except for one thing. I was **still** carrying that rotten financial backpack, I found myself equally as stressed about covering the cost of my kids high school registration fees as I was about covering college tuition that first year of marriage.

Something was seriously wrong! Now I was upset! I was determined to find a way to get rid of that financial backpack once and for all. I was not only going to learn how to get rid of it, I was going to throw it in the chipper shredder, then burn the shreds and bury the ashes. Then, I was going to tell everyone that would listen to me how I did it.

I started pouring through books as fast as my simple mind would process them. I started calling my millionaire friends, I called people I had taught how to fly, people I had worked for in the past, until finally... years later I discovered a formula that I hoped would allow me to get rid of that backpack once and for all.

First I'm going to share with you my current plan which includes this book, a podcast and YouTube. Then I'm going to tell you about some of my failed attempts at financial freedom and what I learned from each of them including why they failed. Finally, I will share with you the simplicity of the secret behind the magic trick of making money.

My current plan includes self publishing this book on Amazon in ebook form. I have included a 10 video YouTube series along with a 10 episode podcast series explaining what is in the book. I have linked all three of them together with affiliate links and internet ads. I'm using social media of all forms as free advertising. I personally will not be handling physical products or processing credit cards.

This plan has taken me a lifetime of trial and error to develop. It has cost me thousands of dollars in failed attempts to learn what didn't work and why it didn't work. I'm leaving you the knowledge of what I've learned. But the wisdom of what to do with that knowledge will only come with time after you decide to act.

The road to success is like approaching the sound barrier. It's extremely rough right up until you finally break through. Once you break through, the air turns smooth and your speed increases with very little resistance. What you are about to learn will put you at the edge of the financial sound barrier. The final push allowing you to break through is up to you. It will require putting into action everything you learn. Only 1 in 9 will do it.

"If you want to achieve excellence, you can do it today, as of this second quit doing less than excellent work."

-Thomas Watson

WARNING! Be very careful not to focus on what you didn't know. It's natural to feel regret for things we would have done differently if we had know better. Learning that we have been doing things wrong causes us to focus on the past. We dwell in the regret of what could have been, or what we might have accomplished if we had only discovered this knowledge earlier. We tend to focus on all the lost years and wasted time. Trust me I understand. I could have saved the family farm or saved my family years of financial stress if I would have known then what I know now. I might have even been able to save my marriage that ended after twenty three years. Why waste another minute with thoughts of the past? No matter how hard you try you can't change it. After you have finished reading this book, go ahead and have your little regret/pity party but don't stay there too long. Remember how valuable the next 60 seconds are. Each of your experiences have something to teach you. Learn from your mistakes and take what you are about to learn and start moving forward.

Generations of Wealth

I'm not going to tell you the same old stories you've already heard about money. Like, anyone can do it if you just set your mind to it. Or, that wealthy people only became wealthy because they are luckier than the rest of the world. The truth is there is an element of luck, or as Warren Buffett calls it *"The Ovarian Lottery"* but ultimately what happens in your future is up to you.

Warren says unless you were born in the town he was, with the parents he had and his same mental wiring, not to mention the same opportunities, we wouldn't have a chance of being where he is today. He credits a great deal of his success to chance or being born when and where he was, and thinking like he does.

It's no coincidence that you are reading this book, the book found you or you found it. Few people will ever have the chance to hear, see, or read what you are about to learn. Lucky? Just consider it your personal ovarian lottery.

A child born in a one room cardboard shack in Peru will not likely have the opportunities or meet the right people helping him accomplish the same level of wealth as Warren Buffett. When and where you are born does, in fact, have an affect on your ability to create wealth. But ultimately you are in control of how you react to life. Whether you stay in the place you were born or if you choose to keep the same friends.

Maybe you decide to move and become friends with wealthy people and learn from them. It's all your choice and you are 100% in control of your future. Replacing your excuses with action is usually all it takes.

My life events instilled in me a great desire to overcome financial insecurity and to share what I've learned with the world.

I spent two years of my life living in Peru. Three months of that two years I had a good friend and roommate named Pablo. I recall the first night in our one room apartment when he got into his bed for the first time. It was covered with a set of sheets with two brown scratchy wool blankets on top. He climbed in his bed and not much later he sighed in frustration.

"How are you able to sleep with these blankets?" he asked.

"They are so uncomfortable and scratchy, it's as if they are full of pulgas!" (Spanish for fleas) he said in frustration. They were full of fleas but that's besides the point.

I looked across the room and could see that he had climbed in bed between the blankets and not into the sheets beneath them.

"Get in between the sheets," I told him.

"The what?" He replied confused.

"The sheets under the blankets, get in between them." I told him again.

He quickly got out of bed and turned down the blankets to see the thin set of white sheets. The sounds he made when he slid between them were similar to a 7-year-old girl who just got told she was going to Disneyland for her birthday.

"It's like a sobresita! (little envelope)" he said happily, causing me to laugh.

"What? You've never seen sheets before?" I asked.

"No. I never had a bed. I slept on a piece of cardboard with straw underneath it all my life," he responded.

I grinned as I watched his reaction to the feel of his new sheets as he climb in between them.

"*Imagine that*" I thought, I never would have guessed that someone would never have known the comfort of a simple $20 set of sheets. My grin soon turned to tears as I tried to sleep, thinking about what his life must have been like, and what other simple little things he must have gone without like a pillow or a blanket.

Being raised in North America and having the chance to live in Peru played a large part in creating my current mental wiring and my thought process in regards to money and life. It did it's job of instilling deep inside me a strong desire to never be financially insecure. This proved to be much harder than I believed it would be. I've seen the problems the lack of money creates, on the other hand I've seen the greatness and good that can be done with large amounts of it and how $20 sheets changed a man's life that day. Not Pablo's life, but mine, and how it affected my perspective of poverty and wealth.

The more I learned about money, the more each layer of programmed false beliefs began to unravel. The greater my understanding, the stronger my desire to end pointless, financial pain and frustration. The pain isn't because we didn't try, its because we didn't know any better.

In my twenty year search for the truth about money, I discovered that **everything I thought I knew about money was wrong!**

Even though you may not have been born with circumstances like Warren Buffett or Bill Gates, you are in control of your financial future. With a few rare exceptions, attaining wealth does take time. It even follows a generational pattern. Let's use my Peruvian friend as an example. To say he wasn't born with money and had very limited opportunities would be a gross understatement. You may know people that have had money their entire life and many of them will say they are self-made millionaires. This is where Mr. Buffett disagrees.

One pattern that typically takes place has three levels. The first level is the accumulation stage. This is the generation that decides to break the poverty chain. Unfortunately they are limited by the most critical ingredient required to achieve true wealth, time.

Pablo may start out working in a factory sweeping floors. He begins the accumulation of money by saving every penny he can. It may take him ten years to get the money needed to start his own business. With a bricks and mortar business it takes roughly five years for it to stabilize and become profitable. In that five years he will learn how to market his products, find the best vendors, learn how to find and keep reliable employees, and get most of his debt paid off helping his business go from red to black.

At this point he is fifteen years into his business plan. This leaves him a possible fifteen more to build and grow his business. Pablo's children begin the second stage of wealth. They grow up in the store helping Pablo with every aspect of running the business. By default they learn the critical lessons required to keep the business profitable. Once the business is turned over to the second generation, they have another thirty years to build the business into something great. The second generation is able to skip the ten year accumulation period and the five years operating in the red. They have a fifteen year head start over the rest of the crowd.

What was once Pablo's small store, now resembles something like Nordstroms or Kohl's department stores. The third generation or Pablo's grandchildren are the benefactors of the previous two generations' hard work. They don't grow up working in the stores and typically don't learn anything about running the business. When their parents move on, they sell the business or run it into the ground financially for lack of understanding about what makes the business successful.

This is just one example of thousands of financial patterns. It's important to understand this the next time you see the third generation spending $50,000 on a birthday party. That fortune didn't just happen overnight.

But you still might hear the third generation say something like "I worked hard for what I have, I pay for everything with my own money."...the money they earned working for two hours a day in grandpa's store in between polo and golf lesson.

The good news is we live in the information age. What took fifteen years before, can now be done in less than two years. More about that in later chapters.

One last story before we get into the truth about money. It's never been about the money, it's always been about time. My studies soon helped me see that true wealth is time, you will never get more of it. The last 60 seconds are gone forever, never to return.

How much was the last 60 seconds of your life worth? I'll ask you this again at the end of the following story. It's a true account of a conversation told from my brother's point of view that he had with my cousin and his wife. It was a few days after the tragic loss of their two year old son.

"I'm so sorry Rick," I said as I tightly embraced my cousin. We let go of each other as he motioned for me to step inside his home, out of the cold. I took a seat on the couch across from Rick and his wife, Jen. It was time I had paid them a visit to offer my condolences for the recent passing of their 2 year old little boy. I brought my eyes up to look at them, studying their pained and grief stricken faces. Both seemed as though they hadn't slept for days. I stayed silent and let my eyes wander around the room. Toys littered the floor, marking their territory of where their only son had once spent many happy days playing and giggling. Jen noticed my staring. Her eyes began to fill with tears.

"We can't bear to pick them up," she spoke softly.

"Any little thing that says he was here… we can't change," Rick added quietly.

We continued to sit in silence for what felt like days. All of us reminiscing on the better days of the past when their son had been the light of their lives.

"I'm so sorry for your loss," I finally was able to say shaking my head slowly. I blinked back a few tears myself as I knew nothing I could say would lift the pain in their hearts.

"No parent should ever experience something like this," I added. Rick gave me a small but sad smile, and then glanced away from me. The silence continued. The room held an empty and lifeless feeling. My eyes went from toy to toy, dampening my mood to know they would never be played with again by the small hands of their little boy.

Sun trailed into the room through the thick window shades, leaving shadows across the floor. I brought my eyes up to meet Rick's. He was staring out the window when his eyes began to water again.

"Look," he said with a tone of sadness in his voice and pointing to the window. My gaze followed his hand to the blinds, they were covered in a thin layer of dust, revealing the tiny fingerprints of their son. It suddenly dawned on me, that little things like this would somewhat seem like a nuisance to a regular human. Toys laying across the house, creating a mess or dust on the window shades. But here in this moment they were something of a completely different value. They were standing as true evidence of the little sweet spirit of their son. He had lived here, he had played and laughed here. He had probably been smiling out the window one day to see that his Dad was just returning home from work, leaving those fingerprints in the dust as he did.

Those little things were reminders that he had lived, and had been on earth experiencing a life, even if it was for two short years. It taught me to not take those times for granted, times when my own kids left their toys out on the floor or their messy fingerprints on the furniture. All of those things hardly seemed significant when placed in this scenario.

"You never know the value of a moment… until it becomes a memory," I let the words hang in the air as tears streamed down our faces.

How much was the last 60 seconds of your life worth? How much are the minutes with your loved ones worth? Yet, you're willing to give them up for the money you earn at your job?

What Do You Truly Love?

Our current mental programing convinces us we love something when we really don't.

"Yes, I may be giving up minutes of my life at work, but I love my job."

You may or may not think this way. Try the following exercise and let's see if you really do love your job.

Imagine receiving the news that you only have 30 days left to live. 30 days and that's It. What would you do in the next 30 days knowing they would be your last?

I want you to make a list of 30 things you would do in the next 30 days knowing you only have 30 days left to live. The first 10 are usually very easy. As you get closer to the 30th you will need to dig deep to finish your list.

Once you have finished your list, I want you to read over it very carefully. You are now looking at a list of what you truly love. Is "go to work" included in your list? If so, you are one of the few lucky ones.

Of all the times I have asked people to do this, never have I seen anyone include going to work on their list.

How do you know you don't only have 30 days left to live?
Why wait to get that kind of news before you start doing the things on your list? Or worse yet, you could die tomorrow never

having done any of them. Live each day as if it was your last because you never know if today is your last day.

Why do we say we love our jobs? Remember career day in high school? You may have had five people show up and talk to you. A police officer, a doctor, a teacher, a pilot, and maybe a fireman. What did they tell you?

"Pick a job you love."

So we think really hard about the five options and settle on the one we think we will love the most.

Before the internet our exposure to different career options was very limited. I searched careerplanner.com and found a list of over 12,000 career choices. I'm sure with that many options you could find something you truly love, but you can't be afraid to fail. All too often we let that little green piece of paper known as money keep us from accomplishing our dreams.

Famous comedian and actor Jim Carrey tells the story of how his father worked a job he hated only to be let go after years of service.

He says, "It's just as likely you'll fail doing one of those other jobs you don't really like. So why not fail doing something you truly love?"

Odds are you won't fail at all because you truly love what you're doing and will do whatever it takes to succeed.

Take one more look at your list of 30 things. Why not make a career doing those things? I encourage you to write down the 30 things and hang them on the wall in a place you will see them often. Make this your new bucket list. In order to make a living doing the things on your list, you will need to understand the rules of money.

90 vs 10

To understand the rules of money you must first understand your current beliefs about money and where those beliefs comes from.

10% of the population holds 90% of the wealth. You may have heard this before. But have you ever asked why?

This was my first question twenty years ago when I began my search for the truth about money. This book is simply what I have learned so far, build on what you learn and leave it behind for the next generation to build upon.

Why is the money distribution so lopsided?

A few years ago when I first started doing live seminars I went into every store in my county trying to find any kind of magazine that was related to money. Money magazine, Fortune, Forbes or even a Wall Street Journal. I couldn't find one place that sold any of them. Why? Because no one buys them. This is the same economically depressed area where if you make $35,000 per year you are in the top 10% income bracket.

People, Us magazine, and all kinds of tabloids on the other hand, are available by the truckload. Seems we are more worried about what Hollywood actors and total strangers are doing than we are about our own financial future.

In one of my live seminars I invite ten volunteers to come up front for a demonstration. I count out ten $1 bills, I hand 9 of the bills to one person and ask that person to stand off to the side. I call this person the 10 percenter. I tell them not to put the money in their pocket because I do want it back. I then ask the other 9 people to gather around the remaining $1 bill and ask them to hold onto it and not let go until I tell them to. I call this group the 90 percenters. I stand back for a moment or two and then I ask the audience.

What group are you in and why are you there?

Have you ever wondered how two people working for the same company, making the same amount of money can have such different financial outcomes or lifestyles?

One person has all the fun toys, the dirt bike, the boat, and a summer cabin in the woods. The other person can't afford to buy macaroni and cheese. One enjoys vacations to the cabin and Disneyland each year. The other works overtime to pay an insurance bill. One enjoys days off with family and friends. The other works a part-time job just to make ends meet. What's the difference between these two people? They both work at the same company making the same amount of money. Why do they have such different lifestyles? Let's assume all other things are equal. They each have two kids, a spouse and live in the same neighborhood.

The number one difference is how they think when it comes to money and wealth. Who do the 9 people holding the $1 bill get their financial advice from? They get it from the other people in the same group holding onto the same $1 bill.

If I ask the group of 9 people what it takes to be rich and wealthy, they will all agree on the same set of rules they believe to be true about money. If I ask the 10 percenter what it takes to be truly wealthy, the answer is very different. The biggest difference between the 90 percenters and the 10 percenters is how they think.

What do the 90 percenters believe to be true about money?

They say things like, "Go to school, it's impossible to become wealthy without a college degree. Use your degree to get a good job. When you get a good job work hard for your boss and when your boss says,"jump," you say, "how high?" That's the way to get ahead in your company. Then, after you've paid all your bills, live below your means, cut back on fancy dinners and movie nights, use the money you save to make extra payments on your debt. After all that, if you have any money left over you should put it in a savings account.

Did I miss anything? Does any of this sound familiar? What do you think? Is this a good financial plan? Who told you about this plan or that it would work? Where did the 90 percenters learn this information from?

Most 90 percenters can't pinpoint a time in their life when they learned what they think they know about money. They know they heard it somewhere, but where? The worst part... they will defend their financial beliefs all the way into financial ruin and bankruptcy.

Who came up with this financial plan?
"THEY" did.
Who are "THEY"?
"Well, THEY say."
I am continually amazed at how many people base life-altering decisions on what "THEY" say.

Brutal truth: If you do what "THEY" say to do with your money, you may never get ahead financially.

9 out of 10 people have these same financial beliefs yet they are still standing in the circle holding onto that $1 bill. Is it working? Is giving up minutes of your life working very hard for a boss making you wealthy? Is your time yours to do what you want when you want to do it? Do you find yourself working

on holidays and birthdays? Who came up with that plan? Can you think of a specific time or place when you learned what you know about money?

Many motivational speakers talk about how we are the sum of the five people we hang out with the most. In the financial world, we are the sum of the eight people holding onto that $ bill with us.

Here's an example of what happens when you follow the 90 percenters financial advice. I asked one of my first officers what he does for fun on his days off.

He said, "Nothing, I'm too tired and I don't have any money. Before this job I liked to water ski, hike, ride motorcycles, and do anything outdoors. My kids liked going to the pool at our apartment, but now that we have moved for the job we don't have a pool anymore."

Prior to working for this *"dream job and company"* he was living life and having fun experiences with his family. Now that he accomplished his dream of becoming a pilot he can't do any of it. He works extra days to make extra payments on his student loans and he's exhausted when he gets home and doesn't feel like doing anything. He gave up a good life for what he thought was the dream.

Note: He's making more money now than he ever did before his new pilot job. Does making more money really fix your problem?

Wouldn't it be easier to ask the one person holding $9 out of every $10 how they make their money before we spend over $100,000 on a college degree?

You would think so but for some reason we don't believe them. We immediately begin to find fault in their methods. We think things like *"It sounds too good to be true"* or *"That's not the way I was taught to do things"* or *"That only happens if you're lucky."* Or my favorite is the nightmare story about someone they knew or heard about that failed miserably at a business attempt or rental properties and was devastated by the financial loss. But they can't recall exactly who it was or the specific details about what really happened because they really didn't know the person at all. They only heard about them. *"Well THEY say."*

As the 90 percenters vomit up their excuses with scarcely a breath, the wealthy stand there with a smile on their face holding $9 out of every $10 listening to us tell them why we think they are doing things wrong. Why don't we ask the one person holding $9 out of every $10 how they make their money?

Even when we find a 10 percenter who's willing to teach us about money, we don't believe what they tell us because it doesn't match our current financial beliefs. We convince ourselves they are lucky and that could never happen to us. None of what they are telling us sounds familiar. We are so convinced of our current financial beliefs we immediately discredit anything that goes against the norm.

What's the norm?

Everything "THEY" say is the norm.

"THEY" are the 9 people holding the $1 bill. Is it working?

"A fool and his money are soon parted."
Thomas Tusser

Did you know 80% of lottery winners file bankruptcy in the first five years? Just because lottery winners have money doesn't change their beliefs about money and what makes people rich. They still have the 90 percenter mindset.

Their first thought is, *"Now I can quit my job."*

The second thought *"Get out of debt."*

They pay off their home, they pay off their cars, they pay off Mom and Dad's home, they might even pay off the in-laws home if they like them. Then they pay cash for all future purchases.

I know what you're thinking. *"What's wrong with what they are doing? Sounds good to me."*

What they are doing is the very thing that causes them to file bankruptcy. I'll explain, just bare with me - and last but not least, they don't do anything that helps their new money grow. I mean come on, why do you need to invest if you pay cash for everything and you don't have any debt?

They are convinced that if they don't have any debt they are free from risk. Even if they pay cash for everything they still have expenses. They have insurance, utility bills, maintenance and repairs on property and cars. The biggest expense of all… taxes. They don't realize they can still lose their home if they can't pay their taxes.

There are monthly county auctions selling people's homes for delinquent taxes. Yes, you can still lose your home even if you don't have any debt.

Here's the problem, they just created a money eating monster. The bigger the house the nicer the car the greater the expenses. More money is needed to maintain their new lifestyle. Paying cash for everything and not having any debt does not stop expenses. You still have bills to pay.

What did they do wrong? They didn't invest in passive income. Passive income is the main ingredient required to maintain that lifestyle and they don't have any. Mainly because they've never heard of passive income.

True Wealth is Time

Definition: *Passive income is defined as money being made each month that you don't physically work for.*

For a couple of years I flew a private aircraft for a gentleman who owned 13 Wendy's fast food restaurants. He would drive to the airport in his Bentley (a $250,000 car at the time) and would complain about what a piece of junk it was compared to the Bentley his wife drove up in ten minutes later.

We would load ATV tires and a large cooler into his plane, then fly them to their five million dollar vacation home in the Bahamas. Do you think he ever managed any of his restaurants? He might stop in once a year just to check on things but he never did any of the work, his employees did it all. This is an example of passive income.

It takes the lottery winner large amounts of money to maintain their lifestyle even without any debt. They still have any number of expense, like utilities, maintenance and repair, insurance, gasoline, food, clothing, and so on.

The thought of passive income doesn't cross their mind, mainly because they didn't know anything about it in the first place. If they thought like 10 percenters they probably wouldn't have bought a lottery ticket to begin with.

With no passive income and the money eating monster gobbling up money as fast as they can spend it, they find themselves refinancing everything just to keep up with expenses. In less than five short years bankruptcy follows. They now find themselves working at Wendy's because they told their previous boss to *"take this job and shove it."* And the new hourly wage can't keep up with the millionaire lifestyle. They end up right back where they started. They sit in shock and disbelief wondering what they did wrong.

"But I got out of debt. I paid cash for everything. I should have been fine. How did this happen? Even my savings disappeared. How is this possible?" cries the lottery winner.

"More money doesn't make you rich, what you know about money does."
Robert Kiyosaki

You're never truly free or truly wealthy unless 100% of your time is yours to do what you want when you want to do it. I encourage you to re-read that last sentence again.

What one thing do you want more of that you believe would make your life better?

I ask this question to most people I meet. I typically get one of two answers. Time or Money. If it's more money you want you will need to give up more of your time working harder and longer hours to get more money. If you quit your job because you want more time, you quickly run out of money and must return to work. In order to be truly free you must have both time and money. But that seems impossible if we think like a 90 percenter.

Again you are never truly free or truly wealthy unless 100% of your time is yours to do what you want when you want to do it.

You may say "Well, my unemployed neighbors have all the time in the world. Are you saying they are free and wealthy?"

No, they may have all the time they want but, they can't do what they want with their time. If they want to go skydiving in Africa it will take money, but they are unemployed with no money.

How is it possible to have both time and money? If I work I have money but no time. What good is a $70,000 boat if on my days off over the weekend it's raining? If I have time I don't have money and I can't buy the boat in the first place.

You will save yourself a fair amount of time if you set aside your current financial beliefs and start with a clean slate. If you're anything like I was I know you won't discard what you currently believe to be true about money. It can't all be wrong can it? Some of it must be true, right? It's hard and scary at the same time to get rid of years of financial programming. That being said I'll continue to prove my point.

The Magic Trick of Making Money

How can I be truly wealthy having both time and money to do what I want when I want 100% of the time? The answer is ridiculously simple.

It's like a magic trick. When you see a magic trick performed it raises the curiosity and baffles the mind forcing you to ask, how did they do that? Truth is, you could spend a lifetime searching for the secret behind the magic trick and never discover how they really did it.

Only after someone like a coach or mentor says, "Look, he had an ace up his sleeve." Or they show you how the rabbit was hidden inside a secret pocket in the hat before the trick began, do you finally realize just how simple the trick really is. Something so small and so insignificant is all that stood between you and the truth.

The simplicity is what makes the truth about money so difficult for us to accept. We don't want to believe that something so simple was all that kept us from true wealth and freedom.

Many people have spent lifetimes searching for the secret behind the magic trick of making money with little or no success simply because they didn't have a coach or mentor to show them the one tiny little thing they were missing. Or perhaps they found a coach who told them they had the secret but they want $3,000 for the information. They chose not to spend the money and it cost them the next ten years of their life searching for the secret.

If the information they have would let you retire fifteen years early or help you to become financially independent in the next five years. How much is that information worth?

90 percenters will spend over $100,000 on a college degree they never use. How many people do you know that are working in the same field as their college degree? However, they have major heartburn spending $200 on a seminar that will teaching them how to turn lead into gold.

What? Lead into gold?

"Impossible! I would never spend money on something so ridiculous, $200 to learn how to turn lead into gold. It's got to be a scam." say the 90 percenters as they write a check for $200 to cover their student loan payment.

Remember, you can't win the game if you don't know the rules.

A few years ago I bought several boxes of lead tip bullets, ammunition for a 22 caliber gun. I paid $7 a box. I sold the boxes after the 2008 election for $55 per box and bought gold with the money. Ridiculously simple right? But five minutes ago you thought *"impossible"* when you read the words, turn lead into gold.

A Different way to Think: The New Form of Gold

"When you change the way you look at things, the things you look at change." - Wayne Dyer

The first step in learning the secret behind the magic trick of making money is to change how you think. One of the most popular and arguably the best financial books ever written is Napoleon Hill's book, *Think and Grow Rich.* He wrote the book in 1937 and later died November 8, 1970. The book has sold over 60 million copies. It still sells 1 million copies a year. To be on the New York times bestseller list you need to sell one hundred thousand copies.

Take a look at the following image. **IX** Grab a pen and paper and copy the image onto your paper. Now using one line, turn the image into 6.

If you've never seen this before, initially your mind thinks roman numerals, that's what you're familiar with. So you spend several moments trying to remember the roman numeral for 6.

HINT: VI is the Roman Numeral for 6. Remember the rule, you can only use one line to turn this image **IX** into 6.

Give up?

Put an **S** in front of the image. What do you see? **SIX**. This is an example of how preprogramming and a little misdirection can hinder your ability to think differently to solve a problem. Using what we think we know can get in the way.

"False evidence appearing real" is what Zig Ziglar called it.
What is meant by false evidence appearing real?

I have a lot of fun with this one. In my live seminars I ask the audience, how good does your eyesight have to be as an airline pilot? I hear the same answer 100% of the time.

"20/20"

"Are you willing to bet money on that?" I ask.

I take my prescription glasses out of my pocket and put them on.

I ask again, "What does your eyesight need to be?"

The looks of confusion are priceless. If you said 20/20 congratulations! You are just like the crowd but unfortunately, just like the crowd you are wrong.

Your eyesight can be terribly bad as long as it's 20/40 with or without corrective lenses. Even then, there are many waivers allowing for exceptions to the rule.

My brother had a crop dusting instructor who had one eye. Can you imagine teaching pilots to fly under power lines with no depth perception? Cover one eye and walk towards a wall. Then imagine doing that at 80 mph and you'll get a small idea of what it's like. Imagine that, a pilot with one eye. Impossible some would say.

"Who told you it takes 20/20 to be a commercial pilot?" I would ask.

One man said "My mom."

"Was your mom a pilot?"

"No." He replied.

Who told you it takes 20/20? *"Well THEY say."* Who are THEY?

"THEY" - are the 9 people in the group holding onto that $1 bill. Remember them? Obviously "THEY" didn't know what "THEY" were talking about. Did you ever ask a pilot if this was true? Did you even look it up online. Today in the information age you don't have an excuse, the answer is in your pocket if you have a smartphone. *"Ok Google."* What are the eyesight requirements for commercial pilots? Go ahead… try it. It only takes a few seconds to get the truth.

When I was young if I wanted to learn something I had to go to grandma's house and look it up in her outdated encyclopedias. If you're under thirty you might have to ask your parents what an encyclopedia is, or say "Ok Google".

It breaks my heart every time someone tells me they would have been a pilot but they didn't even try because they have bad eyesight. They let their dream die because of "False Evidence Appearing Real." Get the truth before you give up on your dream.

Remember, "THEY" haven't got a clue what "THEY" are talking about. "THEY" are the crowd.

"False evidence appearing real or **F.E.A.R.** is one of the biggest reasons why "THEY" fall short of their dreams."

- Zig Ziglar

The Crowd Knows Best, Right?

Years ago Alex - a fellow coworker - and I found ourselves with an entire week in Las Vegas. We had just flown a group of four people from Fort Lauderdale in a chartered private jet for a week long birthday party for a 21-year old girl. We were feeling lucky as we checked ourselves into our free hotel rooms at the Monte Carlo. We had just pocketed $400 each, a tip from birthday girl's Mother.

I did the math, in one week's time including the jet, two $2,500 a night suites in the Bellagio hotel, parties, and booze they spent over $50,000 just for a birthday! Rough life, huh?

Later that evening we decided to walk the famous Las Vegas strip looking for food and entertainment. While walking we were surrounded by a crowd of twenty or thirty people, all heading the same direction, and all looking for the next best place to lose their money. I decided to take the cheap route and not spend mine. I had three kids at the time, and my $400 tip would buy groceries for two months.

If you've ever explored the Vegas strip you know there are several side roads to cross. Most of them with stop lights and the accompanied pedestrian crosswalk signs. At one intersection in particular, Alex and I waited patiently for the light to change, granting us the opportunity to cross. Getting impatient, we decided to cross with the sign clearly alerting us, *"Don't Walk."* I mean come on, we're pilots, there's no stop lights in the sky.

We looked both ways and with no cars in sight, we proceeded to cross the intersection. Directly behind us was the crowd that had been walking with us. They all took the same action, not even looking at the sign. They simply noticed us moving, and as if out of instinct - looking much like a scene out of a zombie apocalypse movie - they followed. We noticed this instantly, and grinned at each other. We had just discovered our evening's entertainment and it was free.

What I'm about to tell you is extremely unsafe and should not be attempted. If you mention to anyone you got the idea from me, I will deny everything. The streets were small, and the speed slow, we were confident we weren't putting anyone in danger.

At the next light, we strategically timed our crossing so we would make it to the other side, but the crowd that blindly followed would be in the middle of the road as the slow oncoming cars arrived. This resulted in the cars having to stop as the small crowd made their way around the cars. It only took a moment before the drivers who were stuck at a green light due to the crowd would blast their horns and wave at everyone with their middle fingers. Resulting in an instant combination of startled screams, people jumping out of the way, yelling and communicating with one fingered sign language.

Needless to say, no matter how many times we did this, the result was always the same. The crowd was never aware, they blindly followed, not ever asking if it was the right time to go or cared to notice the red flashing "Don't Walk" sign. Only noticing the driver's middle finger after being startled by a car horns from three feet away. Ultimately, If everyone else is going, it must be safe to do so, right?

All too often in life we end up in harm's way or in a dangerous financial situation because we too, blindly follow the crowd. No one likes to be singled out, or to go against what everyone else is doing for the sole fear of being wrong, it's human nature. Even with the flashing red lights we discredit all warning signs, convincing ourselves that we must be wrong if we are going against the crowd. Because if everyone else is doing it, that means it must be the right thing.

We've allowed ourselves to become so desensitized, that after seeing the consequences of being in the middle of the road with a horns blaring in our ears, we still choose to jump on the bandwagon at the next intersection, repeatedly.

It's time to wake up, be aware of your surroundings, and pay attention to the signs. Start taking control of your financial future, because everything the crowd thinks they know about money is wrong. They're just following a couple of jokers to the other side of the street who are laughing all the way to the bank.

"When the crowd panics you should be greedy, when the crowd is greedy you should panic."
-Warren Buffett

Breaking Away From the Crowd

The crowd says *"*Hard work and spending over $100,000 on a college education will make you rich.*"*

As a pilot flying in the corporate world, my employers made between $15 and $20 million dollars a year. They weren't doing anything a small town farm boy would call hard work. Sorry, but board meetings and phone calls don't take a tremendous amount of physical effort. Time consuming maybe, but hard work? Yeah right!

The good people back home work very hard from sunup to sundown, often putting in 12 and 16 hour days working on farms or in the dark pits of the coal mines. They make an average of $35,000 a year.

Hard work makes you rich?

I lost a lot of sleep over this one. It's obvious that hard physical labor wasn't the answer. A college degree was also ruled out right away due to the fact that most people in my home town went to college and have a degree of one kind or another.

Look at "Steve Jobs, the founder of Apple Computers" "Bill Gates, founder of Microsoft" "Henry Ford" "Thomas Edison" "Walt Disney" "Mark Zuckerberg, founder of Facebook" "Abraham Lincoln" "Andrew Carnegie, one of the first mega-billionaires in the U.S." "Ben Franklin" "Dave Thomas, billionaire founder of Wendy's" just to name a few. None of them have a college degree of any kind. They are some of the wealthiest people on the planet.

Brutal truth, a college degree has very little if anything at all to do with how wealthy you can become.

We had just leveled off at thirty thousand feet on our way to Los Angeles. The air was calm the sky was blue and inviting like the aqua blue waters of the Florida Keys on a calm day.

I was thinking about the beach we would take our kids to when we lived in Marathon, Florida, when my first officer Justin said, " I just finished my masters degree in finance."

"Congratulations. How long have you been working on it?" I asked.

He said, "two years."

Then slumping over in his seat he asked, "Do you want to know what I learned from it?"

I grinned and said, "sure," wondering how he was going to fit two years of information into the one hour we had remaining before arriving in L.A.

He said, "after all the book work, the studying, arranging schedules around work and school, and the final exams. I can sum it all up in one sentence."

Still grinning I listened as he shared with me the extent of his master's degree knowledge.

"Your outgoing has to be less than your incoming, that's it."

My grin turned into a chuckle. "Justin, how much did it cost you to learn that?" I asked.

He looked at me and in a half disgusted tone he said, "Eighteen thousand dollars."

Without even thinking my comment might add insult to injury I said, "Thanks for telling it to me for free."

I'm not making this up, this really happened. All he took away from his two years worth of work and $18,000 was that you have to spend less than you make.

The best part of the story... for the remainder of our four day trip Justin was reading the book called - *Investing for Dummies* - Again I'm not making this up.

Here's a guy with twelve years of public school, six years of college to include a masters degree in finance and he still hadn't learned the secret behind the magic trick of making money. His master's degree in finance didn't teach him about money it taught him how to work for people with money.

Brutal truth, School won't teach you about money. It will teach to ask "how high?" when your boss says "jump."

Robert Kiyosaki says it over and over again in his book - *Rich Dad Poor Dad* - *"What the Rich teach their kids about money that the poor and middle class do not!"* He has a great video on Youtube called, 'Shooting the Sacred Cows of Money.'

What did they teach Justin? How to work for someone with money. One thousand and one ways to do a resume, how to stand out in the class, make a good impression for the boss, when your boss says, "jump," you ask, "how high?"

I'm sure Justin will be very successful. Even after realizing his $18,000 education didn't give him the answers he was looking for, he still continues to search for the truth about money.

Basic education is crucial and should never be overlooked. But don't be fooled by what "THEY" say, and the dilution that a $100,000 college degree is a requirement to be wealthy. Everything you could possibly want to learn Is now available online and most of it is free. I like to call it youtube university.

The brutal truth about our current educational system is that it's structured to create employees. As employees you don't need to know anything about money, you just work for the people who do.

Why don't they teach us to be business owners and why are we so convinced that owning a business is risky?

If being the business owner is so risky then why do you insist on working for a business owner? How much riskier is it to be the employee?

As a business owner you have options during hard times like, employee cutbacks and downsizing. What options do you have as the employee? Cross your fingers and hope for the best?

Look around you, behind every single object within your field of view is an entrepreneur who started a business. The paper for this book, or the smartphone you're using to read it. The paint on the walls of the room you are in, the chair you're sitting in, the lamp you're using for light, even the light switch on the wall, right down to the tiny screws that are used to fasten the covers over the electrical outlets. All came from a business started and owned by someone who didn't listen to the crowd and wasn't afraid of failure.

If all business fail, none of what you see around you would exist and you wouldn't have anywhere to look for a job.

I challenge you to count how many businesses you pass from your home on your way to work, preferably while someone else is driving.

I interviewed over 100 of my coworkers and asked them why they thought most people don't start a business instead of getting a job for a company. Almost without fail they would say because owning a business is very risky and complicated or they lack the capital to do so.

Who told you owning a business was risky? "Well THEY say."

Anytime I mention owning a business, I'm immediately confronted with "Yeahbuts". What's a yeahbut?

"Yeah but" owning a business is hard and risky.

We hear story after story about failed business attempts, most of them start with, "Yeah but, I heard about a guy that tried starting a business and he lost everything." Or, "my best friend's sister's nephew tried his own business and now he's broke." I could fill several pages with all the "yeah buts" or excuses I have heard over the years and that includes my own, but I'm sure you get the point.

What are you really saying when you say "I don't want to be a business owner"?

I don't want to be a business owner because,

- I will be responsible for the success of the business
- I will have to manage employees
- I will have to manage money
- I will have to organise and plan
- I will have to prepare for the future
- I will have to keep an eye on the ever changing economy.

Think about it. What are you really saying?

You're saying you don't want to do any of that stuff.

- I don't want responsibility

- I don't want to manage employees
- I don't want to manage money
- I don't want to organize and plan
- I don't want to prepare for the future
- I don't want to accept change.

Thinking like this barely makes you employable. You're saying, "I just want to show up to work, do what I'm told when I'm told to do it, get my paycheck and then go home."

But you still expect to be rich?

Personal wealth requires you to do most of these things. If you can't do them at work, what makes you think you will do them at home when you're not getting paid?

Or maybe you're that person who wants to climb the corporate ladder. So you work hard to make your way to the top. Congratulations you made it! Guess what? You are required to get up early, manage employees, manage money, organise and plan for future changes and you are now responsible for the success of the company. If you fail at these things, you lose your job. You're doing everything the business owner was doing before they hired you? Now you're the one putting in the twelve hour days. Where is the owner? Sipping some fruity drink on a beach in the bahamas while you make them filthy rich.

At least as the business owner you have options when confronted with hard times or challenges. As the owner you can make the necessary adjustments when needed. Like, cutting back on employees or how many hours they work. As the employee you have no control over what the company does. If they decide to terminate your position there's nothing you can do about it.

If you are currently working for a business owner, take full advantage of the time to develop the skills you will need to start building your own business. The best part is, you can do it while you're getting paid. Consider it paid training for when you open your own business. You will be years ahead of the game if while working at your current job you became an expert at managing employees and money, or a master planner, and you're able to see what needs to be done for the future or what measures it will take to survive the hard times.

These skills take time to develop and don't come naturally for most of us. But just like with any skill, take it one step at a time and little by little you master each skill. Soon you find yourself at a new personal level having evolved into a greater version of yourself. Personal growth also requires you to overcome the fear of failure and mistakes.

Still think owning a business is risky?

When my daughter was twelve she said to me, "Dad I'm saving money to buy an Ipod."

I said, "that's great, how much do you have?"

She said, "twenty five dollars".

I smiled and asked, "What happens if you work very hard to save the $200 dollars you need. Then after you buy the Ipod you drop it and it breaks?"

I continued to explain, "You're out your hard earned $200. Now you have to give up more hours of your life to earn another $200. What would you think if we take your $25 and buy you something that makes you money every month that you don't physically have to work for? When the asset you invested in makes $200, you can buy your Ipod. Now if you drop it and need to replace it you simply wait until your new asset makes you another $200. While you're waiting you can have fun with your friends doing whatever it is twelve year old girls do."

She answered, "let's do it."

We went online and found a used industrial grade gumball machine for $25. She purchased it and placed it in an auto body repair shop. Her first month she grossed $19 in quarters. Over the next three years that machine made her over $700 and counting. It is quite literally a money mint, it cranks out new quarters every month.

Less than one year later my daughter purchased a snow cone shack and hired her friends to work for her. She spent her summers going to girls camp and boating at the lake with the family. Her friends spent their summer working in a 9' x 5' shack making snow cones. She averaged between $60 and $100 per day.

Warning: Do Not buy gumball machines before you have finished reading this book. Don't forget we are in the information age. The gumball machine and the snowcone shack are industrial thinking businesses.

I call this - **The Gumball Machine Principle** - It applies to all types of investments. The snowcone shack was just a bigger and more efficient gumball machine. Instead of making quarters it makes $100 bills. Same is true with a 90 unit apartment complex. It's just a bigger better gumball machine. With the income from the apartment complex you can buy a new Maserati with a bluetooth link for your Ipod.

One last thought on business. If everyone thought owning a business was risky, and as a result no one ever started a business, who would you work for? If the owner of your company didn't start a business, you wouldn't have your current job.

If you think you're safe working for a large company, think again. According to CNN over **75,114** people lost their jobs in 2016. Most of them from large companies that offer so called job security.

Employee cutbacks by large companies in 2016

Intel   12,000
Ericsson   8,000
Cisco   5,500
IBM   5,000
Microsoft   4,700
Walmart   17,500
National Oilwell Varco   6,000
Dupont pioneer   6,000
Weatherford International   8,000
Bank OF America   8,000
Seagate technology   8,100

    In the modern information age, technology is changing faster than ever before. Your laptop computer is outdated within a few weeks and your new cell phone is old news within a few months.
    Large companies lack the ability to adjust at the rapid pace required to survive the ever changing economy. When compared to small companies they are like large cargo ships -vs- the speed boat size and maneuverability of the small company. The speed boat size company can turn and adapt very quickly to ever changing conditions and technology. Larger companies require drastic measures when a change in direction is required. Employee cutbacks, policy changes, and

budget cuts all require significant amounts of time and energy to implement. Sometimes these changes can take so long that by the time they are implemented it's often too late.

Mistakes and Failures.

"The road to success and the road to failure are almost exactly the same."
                              -Colin R. Davis

Why do we get a bad feeling when we hear the word mistake? Or why do we have a flashback to a high school algebra class when we hear the word failure?

Truth is our social programming requires us to view mistakes and failures as bad. More on that later, but for now let's take a look at the truth about mistakes and failures.

Are you perfect at anything the first time you try it? Unless you have a superpower the answer is usually no. If you like basketball, are you a pro the first time you shoot the ball at the ten foot high hoop? You line up at the foul line you shoot and you miss, it's a mistake right? Or "fail" is what the kids are saying now. But is this a bad thing? Why do we see mistakes and failures as bad? We instantly have a negative emotional response at the sound of the words. Say them outloud right now MISTAKE and FAILURE. Notice that sinking feeling you get deep inside.

Why do we feel that way when the only way to success is through mistakes and failures, there is no other path. Mistakes and failures are positive stepping stones.

The only way to become good at anything is to miss a few shots. Do professional basketball players start out at the top? Are they born with a magical ability to never miss? No, there is no possible way to be perfect without first making mistakes. Mistakes are how we become great or a professional, and failures are the stepping stones that make up the road to success. You can't get there without them. So why are we so afraid of them?

You shoot the ball you miss. Mistake? You shoot again you miss again. Failure? Yes each miss is a mistake but without the practice of making mistakes you will never figure out what adjustments are required to become successful. Our fear of mistakes keeps us from ever trying, therefore we fail by default because we never tried.

Why do we feel so bad when we miss the basketball shot and continue to feel progressively worse with each subsequent failure?

Michael - the neighbor kid who's on the local basketball team - shows up. He continues to make shot after shot, destroying any confidence we had left. We begin the destructive self criticism routine.

We say things to ourselves like, "he's a natural, why wasn't I born like that? I can't do anything. I'll never be that good. I guess I'm a failure, I wasn't meant to be good at basketball."

These are nothing but excuses that keep us from trying again and again until we get it right. We throw our hands in the air in frustration and give up after only a few tries.

"You miss 100% of the shots you don't take." You fail by default if you never try.

Do you give up after the first ten shots and say, "I'll never be a Michael Jordan"? Do you think Michael Jordan was born with some rare superpower giving him an advantage over you?

"I've missed more than 9000 shots in my career, I've lost almost 300 games. 26 times I've been trusted to take the game winning shot and missed, I've failed over and over and over again in my life and that is why I succeed."
-Michael Jordan

I've heard people use these same excuses when talking about their financial situation. They are in a deep financial rut emotionally, continually comparing their financial success to everyone around them. "They are smarter than me, or they are lucky, or everything that guy touches turns to gold." We tell ourselves, "I just wasn't meant to be rich." As if some invisible force is controlling our financial future.

In Malcolm Gladwell's book - The Outliers - he says it takes 10,000 hours to become an expert. Anyone can do anything but it takes 10,000 hours of training and focus to become an expert. How are you going to get 10,000 hours of practice if you never try because you're afraid of making a mistake?

Remember Thomas Edison? 10,000 tries before he figured out the light bulb. Imagine if he gave up after only one or two attempts.

Why are we afraid of mistakes and failures?
"False evidence appearing real, F.E.A.R."
- Zig Ziglar

Ask a group of five year old children a question and see what happens. Most of them raise their hands saying pick me pick me, they are full of curiosity and enthusiasm to learn.

If you've ever spent more than five minutes in a room with a five year old you were probably bombarded with a gauntlet of questions. What is that? How does that work? What's your name? Can I eat that? Is that yours? Can I play with that? They are full of questions about the world, always asking "why?" They aren't afraid of approaching strangers and making new friends. They are constantly running around the room to discover everything about the world.

How do we respond to the five year old? Sit down, shut up, be quiet, don't do that, stop squirming, I don't know, quit asking me questions, just get in line and follow along with everyone else. We immediately begin to destroy the child's creativity and replace it with negative emotions.

After a few years the questions stop, the excitement of learning fades. Fast forward to age seventeen. Now ask them a question and see what you get. Social circumstances have destroyed creativity and independent thought. By the time the student is a senior in high school you can tell them the Earth is flat.

They think to themselves, "*Well I believe it's round but I'm not sure, but I don't want to say anything because last time I said something the rest of the class made fun of me, or the teacher got after me because I didn't study. I don't want to look stupid.*"

If you think this sounds impossible and that no student could possibly be so ignorant as to believe the earth is flat. Search "Google" for the - *Flat Earth Society*.

Just today I had an adult male probably in his late twenties, stop me in the airport and ask.

"Hey, you're a pilot right?"

"Yes," I said.

He asked, "So, is the earth flat or round?"

He was dead serious. He was obviously following the new debate on the internet amongst the specific group of followers that believe the earth is flat. This is how destroying independent thought is affecting the world.

You can get anyone to believe anything if you sound convincing enough. This is also why new high school graduates will give up their summers working in a 6' × 9' snow cone shack for a fifteen year old boss and won't even question their circumstances.

The thought of opening their own snow cone shack and getting their friends to work for them, never crosses their mind. They've effectively been programed to be worker bees.

"Go to work for minimum wage giving up minutes of your life doing what your boss tells you to do when they tell you to do it."

"That's just what you do."

"That's how life works."

This is what the seventeen year old has been told their entire life and effectively believes. Doing what they're told when they're told to do it without questioning why? Why does everyone know the answer to the following question?

When your boss says "jump," you ask- "How high?"
Programming...maybe?

The success of a company depends greatly on its ability to get its employees to do what they are told when they are told to do it. They must convince them that money is more important than time or, get them to overlook the value of time altogether. If not they may very well end up like Andrew Carnegie with 2000 steel mill workers barricading themselves in one of his steel mills refusing to work longer hours for less pay. He hired the Pinkertons who at the time had more guns than the United States military and 9 steel workers were killed.

Our current education system is designed to create employees for the industrialist or the business owners. The current system doesn't teach students to be business owners. They only teach how to be a good employee. They teach 1001 ways to do a resume, how to stand out in the class and make a good impression for your boss by doing what you're told when you're told to do it.

If mistakes and failures are the only true stepping stones to success. Then why do schools punish students when they make a mistake? Remember the dunce cap?

If you want people to do what they are told when they are told to do it. You must first destroy independent thought. To destroy independent thought you must occupy their minds with rote memorization. How many times did you say, or have you heard your kids say,

"I don't know why I am studying this I'm never going to use it in real life."

Companies can't have their employees thinking for themselves. If they do, the employees will realize just how simple the business is to run and they will start their own business and become competition.

In Robert Kiyosaki's book - Rich Dad Poor Dad - he discusses in detail what he calls "The Rat Race."

Most retirement plans are based on a 30-year career. As a business owner you should effectively get 30 years worth of work out of an employee before they retire.

So how do you get a person to stay at a job they hate for 30 years? You create the American dream. What is the American dream?

"Go to school, get a good education, get a good job. As soon as you have a good job it's time to buy a house."

Why do most Americans have the same dream? Have you ever seen the movie called the Matrix?

How long is a typical home loan? It's 30 years by design.

The minute you sign on the dotted line for a 30 year loan to buy a home. You no longer have a choice but to stay in that job you hate unless you want to lose your new home. You are now in what Robert calls the "Rat Race." The way you keep an employee working at a job they hate is to give them debt, 30 years worth to be exact. You program them to believe that their new home is an asset and convince them it's necessary to borrow money for thirty years to pay for it.

Definition: *Asset;* an asset is something that makes you money or puts money in your wallet.

Definition: *Liability*; a liability costs you money or takes money out of your wallet.

In his book Robert asks, "What is your personal home - Asset or liability?"

Does your personal home make you money or cost you money?

Your personal home is a liability. It takes large amounts of money out of your wallet every month. It's quite possibly the biggest liability you have. It's likely your home is costing you more per month than all your other liabilities combined.

Your home takes a monthly payment, monthly interest, sometimes mortgage insurance, HOA fees, maintenance and repair, utility bills, landscaping and landscaping upkeep, not to mention the amount of true wealth lost in the amount of time you spent at work to pay for all the expenses of a homeowner. It also cost you true wealth in the amount of time you spent trying to keep your home from eroding away over the next thirty years.

Drive around a thirty year old neighborhood and notice just how run down the homes are. You'll get an idea of what I'm talking about. The roofs need new shingles the paint is outdated and needs to be redone. The rain gutters are falling off and the water damage to the brick is beyond repair.

If you pay $100,000 for a home and 10 years later you sell it for $200,000 you still can't call it an asset until you do some math. How much did it cost you to live in that home for 10 years?

You need to add up the mortgage and the interest paid over the last 10 years. You must include money spent on maintenance or remodels, landscaping and upkeep, and utilities for 10 years, as well as HOA fees, and insurance, last but not least don't forget to figure in the cost of that second mortgage or home equity line of credit.

Add your total expenses to the original purchase price of $100,000 to get the real number of what it cost you to live in your home for 10 years. If the total cost is less than the $200,000 you sold the home for. Then you can call it an asset. It finally put money in your wallet, if you're lucky you might break even.

The 9 of Hearts.

You can't win the game if you don't know the rules.

      I have a favorite card trick I use to demonstrate how hard it is to win a game if you don't know the rules. I begin by shuffling the cards for everyone to see. I ask for a volunteer to help with the trick. I tell them to say stop whenever they like as I flip through the deck of cards. When they say stop I tell them to take the card that is showing when they said stop. Look at the card and memorize it. Show everyone else in the room the card and don't let me see it. I have them place the card back in the deck and I shuffle the cards again. I give them a fancy speech about the power of the brain and that I'm going to show them how powerful the brain can be. I tell them to focus very hard on the image of the card in their mind. Then I ask them to cut the deck of cards anywhere they like as long as they think very hard about their card. They cut the deck and magically they cut right to the card they had picked just moments ago, the 9 of hearts. To prove it wasn't a fluke I shuffle the cards once again and just like before I have them cut the deck of cards. Over and over again they continue to cut right to their card every single time.

      They stand there with a look of amazement and confusion at the same time while scratching their heads. I can almost see the wheels turning as they try to figure out the secret of the trick. They may spend a lifetime trying to figure out how the trick is done. But all their efforts will be in vain. They will never figure out the secret because of what they think they know about a deck of cards. They may even get a deck of cards of their own and try over and over again to duplicate the trick but will fail over and over again.

I let them struggle with their own minds for a few minutes before I show them how the trick is done. I first show them that every other card in the deck is a 9 of hearts. It doesn't matter how or where they cut the deck they will always cut to a 9 of hearts.

"But why didn't you see the 9s as I flipped through the deck?" I ask. The fact that every other card is a 9 of hearts is only the first part of the secret behind the trick. The second part is that every 9 of hearts is slightly shorter than the rest of the cards. This causes a skipping effect as I flip through the cards. Because they are shorter, the cards get skipped as I flip through them so you never see any of the 9 of hearts. Its ridiculously simple but incredibly complicated if you don't know how it's done.

Everything you think you know about money is the very thing that keeps you from making more of it. It's because you think you know the rules of money much like you know what a normal deck of cards is. Your pre programming is what keeps you from true wealth and riches. Once you learn the real rules of money, you now stand a chance at winning the game. You can't win the game if you don't know the rules.

The fastest way to learn the truth about money is to accept that much like the deck of cards, we have been programmed to believe all the "yeah buts" of the 90 percenters. Everything the 90 percenters think they know about money is wrong. It's time to discover the 9 of hearts.

P + R = 0

How to become a pro at life.

I consider this to be one of life's greatest secrets. **P + R = O**

I first heard of it in Jack Canfield's book - The Success Principles - He called it "E + R = O" I've modified it slightly.

I call it the how to be a Pro formula.

P = Problem or Possibilities. P stands for the problems or the possibilities you face each day.

When you wake up in the morning you are faced with one of two things, problems or possibilities. Normally you don't have control over the problems or possibilities you may face each day. You don't have control over where you were born or what school your parents sent you to as a kid. But you do have control over your reaction.

R = Reaction. R is your reaction to those problems or possibilities.

How you react to life's problems or possibilities is entirely up to you. You are 100% in control of how your react to life. How you react is the only thing that determines the outcome you get out of life.

O = The Outcome you Get. O is the outcome you experience as a result of your reaction to the problems or possibilities you face each day.

Your reaction is the only part of the equation that determines the outcome you are experiencing. It's important to realize, you are the one who has created the outcomes you currently experience. Your physical status, your financial status, even your spiritual status in most cases is a direct result of how you have reacted to the problems or possibilities that you have faced in your life up to this point.

"You are where you are because of who you are. If you want something different you're going to have to change something."
-Jack Canfield

Let me give you an example of what Jack is saying. Two people are walking down a street when they find a $100 bill. Being friends they split the money each taking $50. The first friend decides to buy cigarettes and alcohol with his $50. His **O** or outcome, he ends up drunk and broke.

The second friend buys two $25 gumball machines. She places her machines in the dance studio where her daughter goes to dance class. Each machine nets her $20 per month. At the end of the year she has $480 in her pocket. Not to mention an endless supply of quarters. She will never need change for a car wash ever again.

Both of them had the same possibility of the $50 gift. Each had different reactions causing two very different outcomes.

My brother told me about a friend of his whose parents traded a pickup truck for a bag a wheat during the great depression.

When I first heard this story, I thought, "*I need to buy some wheat.*"

The more I thought about it, I wondered how much wheat I should buy. As I was doing the math figuring out how much the wheat would cost.

The thought hit me, *"Wait a minute, who was the guy that took the truck?"*

He was in the same depression as everyone else. How could he afford to give up a bag of wheat worth the value of a truck? Not only could he obviously afford to give up the wheat, he was able to afford driving a truck in a time when fuel was rationed.

My grandfather told me about fuel stamps from the depression. They would ration how much fuel you could buy using the stamps. Farmers were issued more stamps because of agricultural needs.

What was the guy that took the truck doing that the guy who gave up the truck was not?

I imagine his thinking was much like the 10 percenters of today. The best way to predict the future is to create it. **P + R = O** If you keep doing what you've always done you'll continue to get the same results over and over. To create the future you want, just work the **P + R = O** formula backwards. Determine your **O** the outcome you want. Then decide your **R** the reaction required to deal with **P** your problems or possibilities. Then put your plan into action.

This next story is about a lifelong friend of mine. It's the perfect example of creating a specific desired outcome and the unique thought process that takes place.

Shawn grew up in the same economically depressed area as I did but with one difference, he didn't have a father. His wonderful mother worked very hard just to put food on the table and keep a roof over their heads.

Needless to say Christmas wasn't a very good time for Shawn or his family. He remembers at the age of 12 he wanted the latest and greatest toy for Christmas. He knew he couldn't ask his mother for this gift because of the added stress it would put on her financially. Knowing his problem and knowing that if he didn't do anything, he could predict the future. He knew exactly what was going to happen Christmas morning. He wouldn't get the toy he wanted.

This was his **P or problem.** He thought to himself, what **R reaction** is it going to take to get what I want Christmas morning?

He decided to approach his neighbors about raking the leaves in their yards in exchange for cash to buy Christmas gifts. He made just enough money to buy a gift for his mother and purchase for himself the toy he wanted so badly. Christmas morning came, Shawn got his desired outcome. He created his future. He couldn't do anything about the **P** problem he faced. The problem of his family having very little money for christmas or that he grew up without a father. But he took control over the one thing he could do something about, his **R his reaction** and he created his desired **O - outcome** Christmas morning.

Shawn went on to create his own very successful company in our small economically depressed area. His company was able to support 25 families. His personal family and the families of his 24 employees. He did this in a place where everyone said it couldn't be done. He was generating twenty five times the average annual income in that area with a company he started from scratch. His company slogan is *"**Whatever it takes**"* these three words can be seen on the side every company truck and storefront. It doesn't matter what problems his employees face they know exactly what Shawn will say if they call him with a problem or excuse.

"Do whatever it takes boys, get the job done, do whatever it takes to get the desired outcome for the customer no matter what the problem."

Shawn realized at the age of 12 you don't have to sit there and wait for things to happen. You don't have to accept your current fate or future outcome. You can take control and create the outcome you desire no matter what problems you face. There are many ways to achieve the desired outcome. Even if it means buying your own Christmas gift. By the way, Shawn never spent one day in college.

The best way to predict the future is to create it. Decide what outcome you desire and then do whatever it takes to get the desired outcome no matter what problems you may face. You can make excuses or you can create the financial future you desire, the choice is up to you.   **P+R=O**

LAND OF THE FREE

You may have heard the saying "Born free, taxed to death." It's closer to the truth than you might think.

Do you believe you're free?

On a flight from Minneapolis to Denver, I asked my first officer Daniel if he believed he was free.
"Yes," he said.
Yes is what the crowd says also when asked the same question.
"Why did you take a job working for a large company?" I asked.
"Job security," he said.
What is job security? Truth is, It's an oxymoron. It's like saying jumbo shrimp, they don't exist! But for the sake of argument let's try to define job security.
So what is job security. Three square meals a day, a roof over your head, and maybe medical benefits. Most companies don't offer medical anymore but we will include them in our definition of job security.
A person working 9 to 5 gives up years of their life working 8 hours a day 5 days a week 52 weeks a year for what they call job security.

"Hello Boss, here I am, I will do whatever you tell me to do today."

Following every instruction given by the boss just so they can have three meals a day and a roof over their head.

Now I had Daniel's attention.

"Let's compare your life to that of the prisoners and the local correctional facility," I said.

"What is security for the inmates? Three square meals a day, a roof over their head and better medical benefits than you and I have and their benefits are paid for by you and I by the way. Is the inmate truly wealthy? Can he do what he wants when he wants with the minutes of his life? No, he does exactly what he's told and when he's told to do it. He's told when to eat, when to sleep, he's even told when to shower," I explained.

"What about you? Did you do what you wanted to this morning or did you do exactly what you were told to do when you were told to do it?" I asked.

Daniel sat in silence, he was obviously thinking about our show time or the time we were required to report to the aircraft that morning.

"The inmate spends all day in a 9' x 6' cell 3' feet away from his cellmate," I said, pausing for a minute to let the reality of our current situation sink in.

We were sitting less than 2 feet away from each other in the cockpit. A jail cell 30,000 feet in the sky. His glance of disgust assured me he understood what I was implying.

"At least the prisoner can get up and walk around," I added.

I continued. "The inmate is already in jail. How do they punish him when he gets out of line or breaks the rules?"

"They put him in solitary confinement," Daniel replied.

"Exactly! solitary confinement," I repeated.

For over 8000 years human beings have not been able to be alone. In regards to the inmates, we are talking about the ruffest tuffest people on the planet. You put them in a room by themselves for a few days and they come out whimpering babies.

I asked Daniel, "where do you end up tonight?"

He sunk down in his seat then said, "I end up in a hotel room by myself."

"Solitary confinement," I said.

You can't go home and take out the trash or go to your son's school play. You can't even kiss your wife and kids goodnight.

"Yeah but, I facetime with them," He said.

I started to chuckle. "How does the prisoner communicate with his family?" I asked.

Over the phone through a piece of glass. Otherwise known as facetime.

"Hi kids, happy birthday, Merry Christmas, how was the ballgame? I hope you all had fun today while I was sitting here in my hotel room talking to you through a piece of glass."

As flight crew you don't go home at the end of your work day, you go to your hotel room otherwise known as solitary confinement. You can't see the family or put a bandaid on the scraped knee of your 5 year old. All you can do is wish them luck with a phone call. You communicate with your family the same way the prisoner communicates with theirs. On the phone through a piece of glass. As flight crew you experience your family's entire life through a piece of glass, something we call face time.

If you work a 9 to 5 job. You spend all day in a 9' x 6' cubicle not much more than three feet away from your co-workers. One big difference is you get to go home at night for a few hours. Your's is a minimum security prison.

The advantage we have over the prisoners is, we can still fix our future. We can still change our outcome or the **O** in $P + R = O$ The prisoners future is written down by a judge. Ours is not!

Still think you are free? How much is your life worth? How much does your boss pay you for the minutes of your life away from friends and family? Let let me tell you about Bill Tapay, the
name is fake the story is real.

Bill makes $35,000 a year he views this as a **problem**. He is continually complaining to his boss that he doesn't make enough money. Yet Bill's **reaction** to this problem is he continues to smoke two and a half packs of cigarettes a day and drinks alcohol every weekend.

His current **outcome**, he has been out of work for the last four months due to heart problems. He can't afford the necessary heart medications to keep him healthy. He lives paycheck to paycheck with no true wealth and has no money in savings.

The interesting part - Over the last 10 years at two and a half packs of cigarettes and day and alcohol every weekend Bill has spent over $85,000 just on cigarettes and alcohol. $85,000 in the last ten years. This is above and beyond his normal expenses, like his car payment, rent and food. This means Bill chose to afford the $85,000. Remember the P+R=O formula.

If Bill stays unemployed, $35,000 will soon look more like a possibility than a problem. Let's take a look at what Bill could have done if he viewed the $35,000 as a **possibility.** We will use the same amount of money spent ($85,000) over the same ten year period.

If every time Bill had $25 instead of spending it on cigarettes and alcohol, let's say he buys one gumball machine like my daughter's. In the same ten year period spending the same $85,000 just $25 at a time. Bill would now own 3400 gumballs machines. If these machines averaged $20 per month - $20 is a fair average my niece bought one of these machines and placed it in a girl's dance studio and she makes $100 a month - If each of Bills 3400 machines averaged $20 per month. He would now be making **$68,000 *per month***. Yes my math is right, $68,000 per month.

This is where I start to hear all of the "yeah buts".

"Yeah but, where do you buy gumball machines?"

"Yeah but, that's a lot of work to place that many machines."

You're right, but keep in mind Bill has worked very hard 8 hours a day, 5 days a week, 52 weeks a year for the last 10 years and what does he have to show for it? Nothing but bad health and no money.

If Bill spent a fraction of that time placing and managing 3400 gumball machines he would now be making $68,000 a month or $816,000 per year. He could easily afford to hire someone and pay them $35,000 a year to manage his candy machines for him.

Keep in mind, at no time in this story did we ever change Bill's hourly wage. He never won the lottery, he never inherited a million dollars from his grandmother giving him an advantage over the rest of us. None of the myths about money that the 90 percenters believe make people rich, happened to Bill.

Napoleon Hill explained how vast fortunes are made with small insignificant amounts at a time that most people overlook. In Bill's story his most expensive investment was a

$25 gumball machine. His most expensive product... a .25 cent gumball. $68,000 per month .25 cents at a time.

Vast fortunes are lost the very same way, with small insignificant amounts that most people overlook.

"It's only a dollar" or "it's only .99 cents" or "it's only .50 cents more for the large instead of the medium drink or popcorn."

These are just a few of the ways we rationalise our spending. Rarely will you lose $85,000 all at once. But you will lose $85,000 in small amounts of .25 cents at a time.

To change Bills **outcome** we only had to change the one that Bill had 100% control over and could have done. His **R,** his **reaction** to the $35,000 a year that he views as a problem. Now let's change one more thing. Take out the words cigarettes and alcohol from Bill's story. Replace it with fast food, soda and a candy bar. Ten years later Bills outcome is still the same. No money, bad health and working paycheck to paycheck.

This isn't an anti fast food and candy bar lecture. I'm simply telling you this story to make the point that more money won't fix Bill's problem. We could double his annual income and ten years later he would most likely have the same outcome he has now.

"Money doesn't make you rich, knowing the truth about money does."
   Robert Kiyosaki, author of - Rich Dad Poor Dad -

Large companies know that if they doubled the pay of all their employees two things will happen. #1 They won't see any permanent increases in productivity. #2 In less than a year their employees will be complaining about not making enough money. They know more money won't fix their employees financial problems, but it will destroy the company's bottom line.

Here is the secret inside the P + R = O formula. On the problem side where Bill smokes, drinks and lives paycheck to paycheck. Bill works very hard for money, he is a slave to it. He gives up 40 hours a week 52 weeks a year working for his true master, no not his boss, but the money his boss will pay him for the minutes of his life.

How much is Bill's life worth? Slightly over .28 cents per minute. Bills boss will pay him .28 cents to give up his child's birthday or school play.

Bill says "Sorry son, I can't come to your ball game because my boss is going to pay me .28 cents a minute to miss it."

That is the value we have placed on the minutes of our lives. The minutes we will never see again and will never get back by choosing to work for money.

On the possibility side where Bill owns 3400 gumball machines purchased at just $25 at a time. Bill's money works very hard for him, he is a master of it. Bills time is now his own he can do what he wants when he wants while having plenty of money to go skydiving in Africa. Bill can do this because he has plenty of people willing to give up their lives for .28 cents per minute working for him.

Don't think for one minute that any of this is easy, it will take Bill large amounts of work, time, and money to get his business of 3400 gumball machines up and running. He may very well have to spend another 8 hours a day after his normal work day, building his gumball machine business. Is it worth it? He would now be making $68,000 a month.

Sound to unrealistic? Ok, cut his earnings in half. He is now making $34,000 per month. Still to unrealistic for you? Cut it in half again, he is still making $17,000 per month. This works out to only $5.00 per month per gumball machine.

The Value of Life

How much is your life worth? Add up the total amount of time you spend at work. Include time traveling to and from work and any time spent doing work related projects at home. Round it to the nearest hour.

Multiply the hours by 60 to determine how many minutes you work per day.

If you work 8 hours 8 x 60 = 480 minutes per day.

Multiply 480 minutes by the number of days you work per week.

If it's 6 days   6 x 480 = 2880 minutes per week.
Multiply your minutes per week by 52. 52 x 2880 = 149,760 minutes per year. Divide how much you make per year $35,000 by your minutes per year.   35000 / 149,760 = .23 cents per minutes.

Industrial Age vs Information Age

Warning again... *Do not buy gumball machines until you have finished reading this book.*

We live in the information age. What does that mean exactly?

My parents grew up in the industrial age. They were taught to get a job, work hard for thirty years and maybe retire with a pension and social security. Computers, cell phones and the internet did not exist yet. This was the path to follow if you planned on being an employee all your life.

I grew up in the industrial / information age. When I was in school, computers were still new and schools did not use them. Now I fly aircraft with more computers in them than the apollo rockets had on their way to the moon.

If you have never known life without cell phones or text messaging, then you have grown up in the information age. The information generation.

Unfortunately, the majority of us are still trying to make our living the way our grandparents did. We are using outdated industrial age thinking, it's as outdated as the cassette tape. We haven't evolved with the information age when it comes to making money.

We were forced to evolve with technology everytime we bought a new car. We went from the cassette tape player to CD's then from CD's to a MP3 plug, then to digital downloads and now wireless internet streaming in your car and gps. Every time you bought a new car you had to change how you listened to your music. Yet when it comes to earning money the method amongst the 90 percenters has not changed in the last 100 years. They still give up minutes of their lives for a paycheck.

Blue collar or white collar, It's the same. You are still an employee giving up your life to make the business owner rich. There is no blue collar, white collar It's business owner and employee.

As long as you are working for a boss you are considered a 90 percenter. Even if you make a million dollars a year your time is not yours.

"True wealth is the number of days you can go and maintain your current lifestyle without you or anyone in your family working for money."
                                                                           Buckminster Fuller

With this definition it doesn't matter if you make $20 thousand a year or $20 million a year. In both cases if you lose your job you still have to change your lifestyle. The only difference between the $20 thousand dollar a year person and the $20 million dollar a year person is the shine on the car and the size of the house. Most employees still live paycheck to paycheck.

Today, technology is changing faster than ever. Your cellphone is almost outdated a few weeks after you buy it. If you don't get on board in the information age, you will get left behind.

How cool would it be if a gumball machine existed that you could purchase just one time? You only had to fill it with content one time, then you could duplicate it as many times as you like for no additional cost. You could distribute the machine world wide and it makes you money around the clock 24/7. Sounds pretty good right? Or maybe you're saying it sounds too good to be true and it's impossible. Once again our 90 percenter industrial age thinking gets in the way of progress.

This magical gumball machine already exists. It's called a cell phone app, an internet blog, a digital video course, a podcast, internet webinar, or an ebook.

For every person who owns a smartphone and has paid .99 cents or more to download an APP. That application is someone else's gumball machine, distributed worldwide with the potential to be in every person's pocket.

Instead of .25 cents like the industrial age gumball machines. It's now .99 cents or more each time someone downloads the app. Anyone can own an app, write a blog, host a podcast or write a book. You no longer have to ask permission. You just publish your content and upload it to the world wide web. Everyone has a voice in the information age and the world can hear you.

Here we go again. I can already hear your "yeah buts". "Yea but, I don't know how to build an app." or "I don't know what to blog about." "I couldn't write a book."

Do you hear that? It's nothing but excuses. You either start working or you make excuses. Most of the time it's the same amount of effort. Stop making excuses and start working towards true financial freedom.

"*I don't know how or where to start.*" Well, thirty seconds ago you didn't know about virtual gumball machines either. That's the cool part about the information age. Everything you could ever want to learn is available in a split second via the internet, and the best part - you can leave your wallet at home, most of the information is free.

Start to read the books and watch the videos that will help you gain a financial education. Enough of the funny fail compilation videos or videos of cats falling off of the television. Get something for your time. Start to research passive income ideas or how to make money on the internet. Don't jump into the first thing you see. Spend at least six months doing research before you spend $1 on your new investment idea.

When my passengers decide they want to fly from Salt Lake City to Los Angeles, they don't say "Well I don't know how to fly an airplane," and they certainly don't say, "I guess I'll go to school for the next 4 years to learn how to fly so I can fly myself to Los Angeles." No! They simply go online look for the lowest priced ticket and pay a few dollars to hire the experts to fly them to Los Angeles safely, saving themselves years of work and thousands of dollars in training.

Today it's easier and cheaper than ever before to have someone else build and maintain your virtual gumball machines for you. Scott Fox wrote a great book called - Click Millionaires - it's loaded with valuable insights and references to all kinds of virtual assistants. He also offers a forum to connect with other internet entrepreneurs.

I ran into some friends of mine in the airport one day who had attended one of my seminars. They wanted to tell me about a cell phone app idea they had. They said they had come up with an idea for an app but when they looked online someone else had already done it.

Here's the neat part about the information age, it doesn't matter if someone else has already used your idea.

With the old gumball machine or industrial age thinking we did have to worry about competition. Old industrial age thinkers want to keep their ideas secret for fear of competition. This outdated thinking is not tolerated in the internet world and you will soon find yourself removed from the information age social media groups.

With the physical gumball machine idea, you wanted to keep the idea to yourself. You didn't want someone beating you to a location or even worse putting a machine right next to yours in the same gas station. Competition is very real in the industrial world, not only is your earning potential limited by how many people visit that location, you're competing with other machines in the same area.

Unlike the industrial age mindset, the internet world is incredibly willing to share its money making ideas. With today's information age you don't have competition. Let me explain.

There are millions of apps out there, how can I build one that no one has done? That's the best part, you don't need to. Why try to reinvent the wheel? I recently googled fitness apps, to find 14,400,000 options available. With information age technology and the reach of the internet there is more than enough for everyone. It doesn't matter if someone is already doing your idea. They are not you, and they don't have your personality or your unique ability to explain things.

I once listened to two different podcast, both had roughly the same content and interviewed the same guests. Both of them very successful and very well done. In the end I chose to listen to only one because I could relate to the older host better than the second much younger host. Nothing wrong with either podcast, I just like the style of the older gentleman it was closer to my own personality.

Only you can relate to your personal following. Only you can reach certain people who are looking for the information you have to share with them. With seven billion people on the planet everyone has the chance to create a successful online business.

A ridiculously successful blog may have one million followers, but let's say you have 200,000 followers on your blog. If you publish an ebook and you charge $10 per download and only 1% of your 200,000 followers buy your book, you just made $20,000 in one day. Imagine if 10% of them bought your book.

Suppose you and four of your best friends get together and create an app idea. The idea is to compile 100 of the best cookies recipes and put them into an app for .99 cents. You launch five individual apps but with identical content. The only thing different is the name. Cynthia's cookie app, Breanna's cookie app, Trevor's cookie app, Courtney's cookie app and Jessica's cookie app.

You launch five apps the same day. Same content just different names. At the end of the first month you have 40,000 downloads each. Cynthia had 40,000, Breanna had 40,000, and so on. None of the people downloading the apps bought it from more than one person. 160,000 different people downloaded the same content with different titles. Trevor told his friends and Courtney told her friends and Jessica told her friends about their apps. At the end of the year everyone has made a substantial amount of money.

It's about creating your own following and marketing to that following. You have over 7 billion people to market your idea and personality to.

Let's put that into perspective. If you tried counting one billion people and if you could count one person every second, it would take you thirty two years to finish counting them. If you are reading this in 2018 one billion seconds ago it was 1985. I'll say it again. With almost seven billion potential customers on the planet there is more than enough for everyone to be rich.

Risky Business

When I show up to work I climb aboard a forty million dollar aircraft, it has very modern sophisticated systems and electronics. It's structure is designed to handle the weight of passengers their baggage, fuel and cargo. We depart the runway and climb to an altitude eight miles high and cruise at nearly 600 miles per hour.

In order to fly travelers from Salt Lake City to Chicago it requires a very elaborate system consisting of air traffic controllers on the ground, satellites in the sky, a well trained flight crew, and a vast ground support crew from baggage handlers to fuel trucks.

This system allows us to fill the aircraft full of passengers, pressurize it, depart the runway and climb into the lower stratosphere safely. Is there risk involved? Yes.

Is it risky? No, otherwise the incredibly conservative Federal Aviation Administration the (FAA) wouldn't let us load innocent civilians on board.

You can never eliminate all the risk from any adventure, but you can keep it from becoming risky with the right preparation, training, and education.

What makes something risky? Imagine we are on board an aircraft getting ready to land at Chicago international airport. We are several hundred feet above the ground traveling at a 200 mph approach speed, the landing gear is down and everything is set for touchdown. Now let's take the pilots out of the flight deck and replace them with two random passengers from the first class cabin telling them to land the plane. *"Good luck we're all counting on you."* What do you suppose is going to happen? Yes, we are going to die! What changed?

The system was fine. There was nothing wrong with the aircraft. There was nothing wrong with the controllers on the ground, nothing wrong with the satellites in the sky. The system did its job. So what changed? The education of the idiots driving the bus!

Before you run out and attempt any of the investments or business ideas that you have read about, make sure you get a financial education first. You can call it your licence to fly a business.

I will use the following true stories as examples of learning to fly to illustrate an important point. I want you to understand as a professional pilot I have spent more time in the sky than the average person will spend in a car in their lifetime. I know what I'm talking about when it comes to flying, my proof, I'm still alive after 25 years of flying and so are over 900,000 passengers that I have safely flown to their destinations.

You could read every book ever published on how to fly an airplane. You could watch every youtube video ever recorded on how to fly. You could attend every aviation seminar and airshow on the planet. Even after all that, if you try to fly an airplane without hiring a coach otherwise known as a flight instructor, you are going to die or become seriously injured.

If you've ever looked inside the cockpit when boarding an aircraft and have seen the hundreds of switches and circuit breakers, each one of them is critical to the safety of that flight and it's up to the pilots to know and understand the function of each and every one. It takes years of training and coaching to get it right. If you're missing even a small part of the information your chances of a successful flight are extremely slim.

Does this mean that everything has to be perfect every time? No, many of the systems have a backup system but it is designed to limit the amount of potential mistakes. Don't let over analysis stop you from launching your new business or investment.

Just like aircraft systems, you should also have a backup system in the form of a financial education and by hiring a coach or finding a financial mentor. If you don't pay a coach or mentor, you will pay for your education one way or another. In aviation you can pay with your life or you can do it the easy way and pay for a flight instructor. The choice is yours.

Odds are you may already know someone that can be your mentor or a coach and is willing to teach you for free, if so congratulations consider yourself very fortunate.

Every business venture, or investment has its own set of switches and circuit breakers. If you don't understand the function of each switch or have each switch in its proper place, your business may not survive. A flight instructor seldom has to make major corrections or aggressive maneuvers to keep a student pilot alive. It's typically just very small taps or light pressure on the controls that makes the difference between life and death. These inputs are often so subtle they go unnoticed by the student. But they are the small corrections needed for the flight to be executed safely. A coach or mentor and a basic understanding of the business or investments you are considering is a must for your survival.

More often than not if something looks easy it's because the person doing it has years of experience and has learned from a coach or mentor. The best part about being alive in the information age is the amount of free information available to anyone.

Decide what it is you want, and start the education process, leave the checkbook at home and learn everything you can about you future business or investment. Use the Internet and the library to get a good understanding of your business idea using the free information available to you. This way when it comes time to hire a coach you will be educated enough to know what questions to ask and what skills and qualities to look for in a coach. After all they are working for you, they may have the information you need but you can still interview them before deciding to hire them.

I have two real life experiences to share with you that illustrate the importance of a flight instructor, education, and training. They involve close friends of mine, they are true accounts of friends I nearly lost.

Jim had just finished building a KitFox aircraft, it's a small two seat homebuilt airplane kit very popular among the recreational private pilot group. His particular aircraft was a taildragger type plane. This means it has a three wheel configuration with two wheels in the front and a small wheel on the tail of the aircraft. Different from conventional tricycle gear aircraft with one wheel in front and two wheels in the back. The tailwheel of the taildragger aircraft is used for steering and control on the ground. It's an old design and requires a great deal of extra training to master the taildragger technique.

Jim, who did hold a private pilot license, had just spent $30,000 and one full year building his kitfox aircraft. When it came time to fly it, Jim refused to get the proper taildragger training because of the additional cost for the instructor. I insisted multiple times that he should get the required training. I tried to explain how common sense doesn't work in the aviation world. It takes precise training and experience to understand the aerodynamics of a taildragger. The Federal Aviation Administration even requires a specific endorsement for taildraggers because of the additional complications and flying characteristics of the aircraft.

No matter how much I tried to explain this to Jim, he insisted that he could figure it out on his own. He would argue with me about how what I was saying didn't make sense to him with his current understanding of airplanes.

"I know it doesn't make sense Jim, that's what I'm trying to tell you," I would say.

I pleaded with him not to try and fly his plane alone and offered my services as a flight instructor for free.

"I don't want to see you die Jim," I said.

He reluctantly agreed to wait for a day when the two of us could fly his new plane together.

Our first flight was fine other than Jim had mounted the radiator - used to cool the engine - next to the extremely hot exhaust manifold. He had done this because the location recommended by the manufacturer didn't make sense to him. The engine was overheating and we returned to the airport and landed before it became a problem. I told Jim to fix the radiator problem then call me when he was ready to try it again.

While I was away at work, Jim decided he was going to try and fly his airplane by himself. Still not understanding the aerodynamics of the taildragger design he was able to take off without incident. The landing on the other hand didn't go so well. Upon touching down on the runway the tail wheel was tossed sideways because of over control inputs by Jim. He lost control of the aircraft. It pitched sideways turning a hard left and sent him off the edge of the runway. Jim and the aircraft came to a stop in the tall brush that lined the edge of the runway as dust and dirt from the impact filled the air. The aircraft had ended up with its nose and propeller in the dirt breaking the propeller and causing damage to the front engine cowling. Luckily, Jim was unharmed, other than a bruised ego.

After hearing about his accident I called Jim and told him to call me when he had his airplane fixed and I would teach him how to fly it. Again he agreed.

A month or two had gone by and I hadn't heard from Jim. I decided to visit him at his home. After some small talk I asked if he had repaired his plane yet.

He said, "yes but I crashed it."

"I know you crashed it, but did you fix it yet?" I asked again.

"I had fixed it the first time but I crashed it again."

"What! You crashed it again?"

"Yes," he said.

He was so convinced he could figure it out that he refused to call me and take advantage of the free instruction offer. He wasn't convinced that I knew what I was talking about when it came to taildragger aircraft.

He said "I've taught myself everything. How to play the guitar, how to ride a dirtbike, and how to install solar panels on my home. I figured I could teach myself how to fly a taildragger. I watched the videos before I went."

"None of those things will kill you if you make a mistake Jim," I said in frustration.

"An airplane will kill you when you do something wrong. You can't just hop in and think things will be ok if you screw it up," I said with a slightly louder tone in my voice.

His second crash was on landing like the first, only this time he ended up completely upside down on the side of the runway. Breaking the wings and tail off of the fuselage of the airplane. Totally destroying his $30,000 KitFox with less than 3 hours flight time on the brand new aircraft. It never flew again. Jim was uninjured but lucky to be alive.

My second friend wasn't as fortunate as Jim. His story was very similar with regards to not wanting to pay for flight instruction. Randy had flown with me several times In my personal Citabria, a taildragger aircraft capable of aerobatics. I told him I would take him anytime he wanted to go flying.

He was bitten with the flying bug and decided to look for an airplane to buy for himself. Randy, unlike Jim did not have a pilot's license or training of any kind. He was very mechanically inclined and operated many different kinds of heavy equipment. His mindset was much like Jim's. He thought flying looked easy enough and thought he could figure it out on his own with no instruction and only using videos he found online.

As soon as I heard about his intentions to buy a home built aircraft he had found online, I called him immediately. The conversation almost cost us our friendship.

His last words to me before he hung up on me were, "Why should you have all the fun?" Click.

I called him back and said, "Randy, it has nothing to do with me not wanting you to have fun. I don't want to go to your funeral."

I had to insist on making him upset at the cost of our friendship because he wouldn't listen to reason or to his friend who flies aircraft for a living and has done so for 25 years. This is a typical mindset caused by lack of money.

Sadly enough he didn't listen to my advice and the advice of other pilot friends. He attempted a flight with no instruction and crashed, crushing the right side of his head and body. He spent just under four months on life support in a coma. He eventually woke up but is now crippled and suffers from severe brain trauma. He will never be the same again.

Both of my friends stressed about money most of their lives, the lack of money nearly cost them their lives.

They failed to see however just what it was going to cost them by not getting the training required to save their life. Flight instruction for Jim was offered for free yet his stubbornness and lack of education cost him $30,000 and almost cost him his life. He didn't have insurance on the aircraft for the same reason. "Insurance cost to much," he said.

Randy lived but lost his life as he knew it. He paid a much greater price and so did his family who depended on him as an only source of income.

I share these true stories in hopes that you will see the importance of getting a financial education and training before you attempt any business venture. The training will be much cheaper than the devastation of the failed attempt. Every business has just as many switches as the jets I fly. You need to learn about all of them before you attempt to fly the business of your choice. You don't need to master them before you attempt your business but you do need a basic understanding of each level of your business and have a coach or mentor available when you have questions. Find the expert and let them help you fly your business to success. Learn to trust them and follow their instructions even if it doesn't make sense to you at the moment. Be patient it will all be clear soon enough. It will save you years of trial and error and thousands of dollars in the long run. The financial devastation from lack of understanding can be equally as damaging as the physical injuries sustained by my friends. Money or lack of it has been been attributed to an alarmingly high rate of divorce and suicide.

"The man who keepeth in his purse both gold and silver that he need not spend, is good to his family and loyal to his king.

The man who hath but a few coppers in his purse, is indifferent to his family and indifferent to his king.

But the Man who hath not in his purse, is unkind to his family and disloyal to his king, for his own heart is bitter."

-The Richest Man in Babylon: By George S. Clason

Duplex

The 90 percenters typically say "investing is risky." Yet they live in the riskiest way possible. They go to school and get a good education to get a good job. If they find a good job they naturally want to start living the American dream of owning a home. The cost of a new home makes it nearly impossible to pay cash so they finance their new home using a typical 30 year mortgage. They can't be seen driving their old beat up college car to their new fancy job so they borrow money to buy a new car. I mean hey why not? They can afford the payment now right? Their spouse doesn't like the look of the milk crate furniture they had in their college apartment. So they head down to the local furniture store and buy all new furniture using a credit card. It's only $100 a month so why not? No one will see them as successful if they don't have some kind of new toy to show off. They decide to buy a new side by side atv or all terrain vehicle. What's another $20,000 in debt?

"No big deal," they say, "It will be worth it, think of all the fun we will have."

That's what they tell themselves to justify the expense. Now that they have the new side by side they need a trailer to pull it. If you have a trailer and a side by side you need the new jacked up, souped up, hopped up, chromed up, diesel pickup truck to pull it right? I mean, you can't get by without one it's a necessity now. Right?

Within a few short months they are living paycheck-to-paycheck. Everything they own is dependent on their ability to earn money at work. If they get in an automobile accident rendering them physically unable to work, they lose their job and in turn they lose everything. Everything they think they own goes right back to its rightful owner, the person who lent them the money. It doesn't get any riskier than that.

Everything they own is dependent on one source of income. If they are lucky enough to have two incomes typically the lifestyle is more than one income can handle and they are forced to downsize everything.

They can't sell the truck because they owe more than it's worth. They can't return the furniture to the store, they won't take it back. They sell the side by side at a terrible loss. Next they are forced to look for a new smaller home to rent. Can you think of anything more risky than this scenario? Unfortunately 90 percent of the population lives just like this.

Take a look at two friends Mike and Lucy. They both work for the same manufacturing company. They've both worked at the company for eight years. They make the same amount of money doing the same job. Both Mike and Lucy make a gross income of $3,000 per month.

Mike lives in his new home with all the toys, a new car, boat, and motorcycle. He bought his home for $100,000 with a $650 a month payment. He also has several small loan payments for all the toys.

Lucy goes to the same bank and asks for the same $100,000 loan. But instead of buying a home she buys a duplex. She has the same monthly payment of $650 per month. She rents out both sides of the duplex. Charging $750 per side for a total of $1,500 per month gross income. She uses the rent money to pay the loan payment of $650 leaving her a net income of $850 per month.

Mike, with his home and all his toys makes the same $3,000 a month as Lucy but he spends approximately $2,800 a month on loan payments. Leaving him with $200 at the end of the month.

Lucy is making the same $3,000 but has a duplex making an extra $850 per month. She pockets a total of $3850 per month. Not one penny of her $3,000 paycheck is going to debt payments. Not even for the duplex.

Mike heard about Lucy's deal and at first he thinks it sounds like a great idea. Mike goes to the bank and asks for another $100,000 loan to buy his own duplex.

The banker promptly says "No."

Why? Debt to income ratio.

Debt to income ratio is based on loan payments not the loan amount. If Mike has a $100,000 loan but the monthly payment is only $50 per month. The bank will lend Mike more money. They will keep lending Mike money until his monthly payments equal 33% of his gross income. With Mike's home loan and all the toy loans he's over the 33% debt to income ratio limit. This is based on his income of $3,000 per month and his $2,800 per month in loan payments, Mike is maxed out. He's living paycheck to paycheck. He's doing fine as long as he has a job and makes enough money to make the payments on all his debts.

Lucy still needs a place to live. She rented the duplex to a couple of nice families that pay her on time each month. She knew they would because she did background checks on them before signing the rental contracts.

Lucy heads down to the bank and asks for another $100,000 loan. This time she's going to buy a personal home with the money.

The bank says "yes."

Why? What is Lucy's debt to income ratio? Zero! How is it zero? She had a loan of $100,000 on her duplex. How much of Lucy's $3,000 paycheck is being used to pay debt? Zero.

The duplex is making its own payment using the rental income, not Lucy's earned income from her job. Not only is the duplex making its own payment it's putting an extra $850 per month in Lucy's pocket. She can show the banker a $3,850 income. Unlike Mike who can only claiming $3,000 per month with $2,800 in expenses.

Lucy, gets the loan and buys a nice comfortable home for $100,000 with a monthly loan payment of $650. When the rent checks from the duplex come in, she uses $650 to pay the duplex loan. She uses another $650 to pay her new home loan payment. She still has $200 left over. She puts the $200 together with her $3,000 paycheck from work and still has $3,200 dollars at the end of the month after all her bills are paid.

Mike has $200 left over and he uses it to make extra payments on his debts.

Since the bank told Mike "no" when he asked for a loan to buy a duplex, he's change his mind about investing being a good idea. He now says what Lucy is doing is risky.

Let's recap.
Lucy has $200,000 of debt.

$100,000 for the duplex
$100,000 for her home.

She's has two $650 per month payments. One for her home the other for the duplex totaling $1,300. She has two rental incomes of $750 each from the duplex for a total of $1,500 per month. Leaving her an extra $200 per month. She also has her $3,000 per month income from her job, placing a total of $3,200 dollars per month in her pocket. She could easily afford to pay cash for all the same toys Mike has since she makes an extra $38,400 per year above all her expenses.

Mike, makes the same $3,000 as Lucy. But he spends $2,800 per month on loan payments with no other source of income. He has $200 at the end of each month he can pocket or pay towards his debts. Who would you rather be?

They both started out with the same income but ended up with very different outcomes.

Mike and Lucy decide to carpool to work one day. They get in a terrible accident and both are badly injured. Their injuries are bad enough that neither Mike or Lucy will ever work again.

What happens to all their stuff?

Let's look at Mike first. He can't pay the loan on his home, the side by side or the new car. He can't make the payment on the credit card he used to buy furniture for the new home. What happens to all of Mike's stuff? He loses everything. He even sells the furniture to pay off the credit card. Mike is out on the street with no money and no place to live.

What about Lucy? The duplex is still making its own payment and it's making the payment on her home as well. She even has $200 a month leftover to buy groceries. No one can tell that Lucy doesn't have a job anymore.

Mike sees that Lucy is still in her home and she still owns the duplex.

"How can that be?" he says.

"She lost her job the same day I did, how can she still afford her home and duplex?"

"She's got to be doing something illegal," he exclaims.

"I'll bet she's growing weed in her basement," says Mike's wife.

Mike and his wife are still thinking like true 90 percenters. They don't know about the 9 of hearts.

Are the Rich Luckier than the Poor?

I wish I had a dollar every time I heard someone say "Yeah but, the rich are lucky."

Funny enough, when I've asked wealthy people how they got where they are, most of them say with a grin "I was lucky".

I soon discovered the rich have a very different definition of luck than the rest of world.

One of my favorite ways to finish a live seminar is to hold up a ten dollar bill and ask who would like this ten dollars. Almost everyone raises their hand indicating they want the money. I look around the room waiting to see who really wants the money.

The arms get higher and the pleas get louder saying "pick me, pick me!"

I tell them, "I see many hands in the air but I still don't see anyone that wants the ten dollars."

Finally after several minutes, Someone gets up off their chair and comes up to get the money.

When I give it to them, what does everyone in that room say about the person that received the money?

"That person is lucky!"

Everyone in that room had the exact same opportunity to be $10 richer. Anyone of them could have gotten up and taken the money. (P + R = O) Only one of them took advantage of the opportunity while the rest just sat there.

When the rich say they are lucky. They are talking about how lucky they are that no one else in the room stood up to get the money.

"Really!" They think to themselves, *"I'm the only one that can see this opportunity? I just made ten dollars for nothing and not one other person tried to claim the prize."*

All It took was a unique way of thinking that is different from the crowd.

The opportunity of a lifetime passes you by every day.

Let me tell you about another friend of mine named Stacy, a 62 year old flight attendant from Brazil. Each time I fly with Stacy I can't wait to hear what new project or business deal she has going. She is always smiling and loving every minute of life. To see her you would never guess that Stacy is a millionaire. She is truly wealthy in both time and money.

Stacy took the flight attendant position as a retirement job allowing her to travel the world for free even though she could easily afford the price of a ticket. Her husband worked most of his life for a well known hotel chain allowing them to get free hotel rooms when they travel.

Years ago - before becoming real estate investors - Stacy worked at a company that gave her stocks as part of her compensation.

The last time I flew with her she stuck her head in the Flight Deck and said "Hey Todd, Do you remember those stocks I told you about the last time we flew?"

"Yes" I said.

"I checked them last night and they are worth over one million dollars." She said with a very large smile.

I remember thinking at the time the stock market wasn't doing very well and I said "Stacy, why don't you cash them out?"

"Yeah, I don't care, I don't need them and I would like to see how much they will be worth in a few years."

Yes, I felt the same as you do... How would it be to have an extra million dollars you didn't need?

As I was writing this story I took it to Stacy for her approval. She told me her stocks are now worth over two million dollars.

Stacy and I were flying with a first officer who was working on his bachelor's degree. He had finished his first two years of college and was working on his third year. He said it was so he could get hired on at a major airline. He also volunteered additional information stating that he and his wife were trying to have a baby. Almost in the same breath he said his wife had quit her job and told him he needed to make more money.

"So you're expecting?" I asked.

"No she just quit her job and said I need to make more money," he said with a disgusted tone.

Just then Stacy returned to the flight deck. "What new deals are you working on Stacy?" I asked.

Stacy and her husband had owned several rental properties in a number of states in the U.S. They had sold most of them but still maintain a few investment properties. Mainly because of old habits and the investor mindset, a good deal is still a good deal even in retirement.

"We have a two bedroom one bath condo in Centerville. We are getting $1,800 per month," she said.

"What? How are you getting that much?" I asked.

At the time $1,800 was well above the average rent for a two bedroom condo in Centerville.

"Centerville is growing very fast right now. Many large companies are building there like Walmart, Texas Roadhouse and Target," Stacy continued to explain.

They send executives to oversee the projects and they stay for several months at a time. The executives show up at the hotel where her husband works and ask how much it will cost to rent a hotel room for the month.

He looks it up and says "$3,400".

He waits a few seconds to see the look of shock on their faces.

Then he says "I have a two bedroom condo fully furnished you can rent for $1,800 a month and I will let you rent it on a month to month basis."

She said, "The checks come from the corporate offices and they always pay on time."

"How often does it go empty?" I asked.

"Never, we have a two year long waiting list the corporate offices call me directly. The only time it was empty was when one gentleman rented it for two months and never showed up just because he didn't want to lose it to someone else."

I couldn't sleep that night in the hotel. I was too busy looking up real estate listings in Centerville. I found two listings for two bedroom one bath condos. One for $80,000 and the other for $84,000. I spent most of the night calculating numbers and return on investment for the two properties.

A little bit of self disclosure here, I was driven by the fact that I had just closed on two rental homes within the previous two weeks and I wasn't going to make near the return that Stacy was making on her one condo.

The next morning I arrived at the aircraft with a bunch of questions for Stacy and a full set of real time numbers showing the income the two condos could generate.

"Stacy, how many calls do you get where you have to turn people away because your rental is full?" I asked.

"I get calls daily and like I said we are booked for the next two years." She replied.

"Would you be willing to send those people to me or someone else who might buy a condo in Centerville?" Was my next question.

"Of course." She said with the same tone and carefree attitude as when I asked why she didn't cash out her million dollar stocks.

She obviously didn't see it as competition and knew the niche market she was in could easily handle a dozen or more of these types of rentals. Rentals that allow a month to month rental contract.

Remember the first officer whose wife had quit her job? I immediately started to show him the math on the two properties. But before we get into the numbers let's take a look at his current plan.

His wife just quit her job and told him he needs to make more money, and they are trying to have a baby. His plan is to spend the next two years finishing school. Then upgrade to captain and start building pilot in command time that is required to even apply at the major airlines.

The national average for college tuition is $29,000 per year. The minimum upgrade time at our airline was seven years. At the time of this story he had been at the company for two years. It would be another 5 years before he can upgrade to captain and at least one year as a captain building his flight time requirement.

He's looking at a minimum of six years and $58,000 before he can apply to a major airline with no guarantee he will even get the job and they're going to add a child to the mix.

Sadly this is normal thinking for 90 presenters. The minute most people lose their job their first thought is to go back to school and spend more money they don't have.

The first officer had been listening to the conversation between Stacy and I the day before. I wanted to show him the numbers on the rental properties. I had calculated everything with traditional financing and a 20% down payment. In my calculations I used his absolute best case scenario. I figured a conservative $16,000 per year instead of the $29,000 average for college tuition for a total of $32,000 for his final 2 years of school.

His plan is going to take him a minimum of 7 years to complete. I'm going to use a best case scenario of 4 years.

Even if the stars aligned and all of this happened, he would still take a pay cut his first year at a major airline. In his second year he may break even and make as much money as he did at his previous job. Don't forget he is still $32,000 in the hole from school. Whether he borrowed the money for school or paid cash is irrelevant he is still out $32,000.

I'm not quite sure what his wife thought of his plan. But it's certainly not going to help them in the short term. They have an immediate pay cut since she just quit her job.

Just to reiterate he's looking at a minimum of 4 years best case scenario before he sees a pay increase of any kind and at that point he still has to recover the $32,000 he spent on college. Again this is best case scenario. Real world is minimum of 7 years before any of this happens for him.

As we waited for our passengers to arrive I told him about the two homes I had found for sale in Centreville. I told him one was listed for $80,000 and the other one was listed for $84,000 both of them currently available. I began to show him the numbers.

The first condo is listed for $80,000
20% down payment = $16,000
Loan amount = $64,000
Investment loan interest = 4.1%
Monthly payment = $309.25
Management company = $150
HOA fees = $150
Taxes = $50
Maintenance = $25
City fees =$65
Vacancy = $50
Total cost per month for hands off operation = $799.25
Rent = $1,800
Net income per month = $1000.75

    Using real time numbers and including all expenses required to run the rentals hands free using a management company, I was able to show him how he could clear a $1,000 net profit per month per home.

    I said, "take the $16,000 you will spend on your third year of college and use it as a downpayment on that first condo.You could close the deal and with Stacy's help, have it rented within a month. If you do this you will give yourself an instantaneous $12,000 a year pay raise. Use the money you would spend on your final year of college and do the same thing with the second condo. You are now making $24,000 extra per year and not doing anything for it."

I asked him "how much are you making right now?"

"Gross is just under $40,000. Take home around $30,000 per year." He said.

"Ok, stay at the company for one more year after you buy the two condos. Your condos will net you $24,000. Use the $24,000 for a downpayment on a third condo." I said.

"You are now netting $36,000 per year, $6,000 more than you currently make giving up minutes of your life all year long. And what are you doing to earn the money? Nothing! They are managed for you and your time is 100% yours to do what you want when you want to do it. In one year's time you would net $36,000 passive income, you could quit your job, go home and make that baby with your wife." I said with a smile. 1 year vs 7 years for a maybe job?

Every time we flew over a large city like Los Angeles or Denver I would say "Just think, three of those homes and you could quit your job."

His only response was a disgusted glance at his school books.

The point of this story isn't to get you to run out and buy rentals. Don't do it without the proper training. The point is, this was a very niche market but very possible. He had everything he needed to take advantage of the very unique market. He had home availability and he will spend the same amount of money he'll spend on school. He also had the most important part, a coach named Stacy, who is more than willing to help him.

The opportunity of a lifetime passes you by every day. Most of the time we never see it. Every flight crew member that had flow with Stacy over the past few years had the same opportunity to jump into that unique rental market. I would be willing to bet, we were the only ones to have discovered the opportunity in that way. Lucky? Maybe. I guess you could call it lucky that we could see it and no-one else did.

Opportunities like this pass us by everyday but seldom do we recognize them or we're not in a position to take advantage of them. We are so focused on our job and doing what everyone else is doing, that we never stop and do the math to see if our plan makes any sense.

In order to recognize opportunities we need to be actively searching for them. I ask everyone I fly with if they have any side business. That's how learned about Stacy's story. I never would have discovered that opportunity if I didn't think the way I do. We probably would have simply discussed the weather or what fun things we had planned for summer vacation. The opportunities are all around us, we must learn to see them.

Don't waste time trying to come up with an idea out of thin air. What typically happens after I introduce this information to someone new is, the following morning they say,

"I was up all night trying to come up with ideas for passive income and all I could think about were gumball machines."

Keep in mind it is extremely rare to come up with a truly original idea out of nothing. In fact if you do you will most certainly become a billionaire. An example of a truly original idea is the internal combustion engine. What is it used for? Everything from cars, boats, trains and planes and in any mode of transportation imaginable. It's not likely that you're going to pull that idea out of thin air by locking yourself in a room for hours on end. Most truly original ideas evolved out of a chain of events. The book - Seeing What Others Don't - by Gary Klein disguises in great length the theory behind insights.

A quick story about insight. In 1905 Kansas was plagued by an overabundance of flies. Dr. Samuel Crumbine from the Kansas board of health, had discovered that flies were widely responsible for spreading germs and communicable diseases. The problem he faced was how to get rid of the flies. At first his recommendations were to keep the flies out of homes with screen doors and windows.

Later while he was at a local baseball game the crowd was chanting "swat the ball" he was inspired to swat the flies. It would be more effective to kill the flies than to keep them out of the homes. He published a bulletin inspiring citizens to "swat the fly." This inspired a group of boy scouts to attach screen to a yard stick. It was left over pieces of screen they had helped place on the communities doors and windows. They originally called it the "fly bat." Dr. Crumbine said "No it's a flyswatter."

The need for a cure to the spread of diseases + ball game chant "swat the ball." + helping the community install screens on doors and windows + leftover screen attached to a stick = Flyswatter.

An idea that evolved out of a series of events that started with disease control efforts. It's not likely that anyone would have just pulled this idea out of thin air. It is possible that you may be the next person to come up with a world changing idea if you are attuned with the sequence of events that lead up to that idea. Keep your eyes and mind open.

The secret to coming up with new ideas Is known as networking. The people you associate and work with the most have a tremendous effect on your ability to come up with new ideas. Your network (the people you associate with the most) equals your potential net worth. The following story is an example of how my personal network of friends allowed me to start my own sea salt scrub business. It evolved out of a simple phone conversation that lasted about 5 minutes.

The phone call took place during my 2 hour drive to work. I had called a former flight student of mine who's a very successful business owner. I was calling to ask him about opening a boat dealership, he had owned one while I was living in the Florida Keys. As I asked him about opening a boat dealership, within two minutes he told me it was a bad idea.

He said, "luxury item in a bad economy, bad idea."

I knew he knew what he was talking about, I didn't waste another minute entertaining thoughts of a opening a boat dealership. I did ask him if he had any ideas for some kind of business I could start to help ease some of the financial burden I was experiencing at the time. He said he couldn't think of any at the moment.

We chatted for awhile about normal stuff like the weather and how each other had been since the last time we seen each other. It had been several years since he had learned to fly and he paid for my first ever skydive as a gift for helping him complete his pilot's license.

Nearing the end of our conversation he said "Oh, wait a minute I do have an idea for you."

He proceeded to tell me about a sea salt scrub that is used for washing hands and exfoliating the skin that he sells in his restaurants. It's made with an old recipe that came from fishermen in the Florida Keys. They would use the scrub to remove the fish smell from their hands. He proceeded to tell me how they make it, how much it cost for a jar and how much he would sell it for.

"I will email you the recipe," he said.

The sea salt scrub itself was an amazing product and worked very well, but that wasn't the great idea. The great idea was how he told me to market the scrub. Like I said, he sells it in his restaurants.

If he tried to sell the scrub in a store like Bath & Body Works it would be competing with a minimum of 30 different types of scrubs already on the market but, he sells it in restaurants.

Who would have thought of trying to sell a hand scrub in a restaurant? How does that work? He told me to approach restaurant owners and ask them how much money they make from their restrooms? The answer is always "nothing" in fact it is a very large expense for restaurant owners. They provide the restroom facilities to their customers free of charge. It cost them a great deal of money in supplies like paper towels, someone to clean and maintain the restroom, toilet paper, and utilities like water and electricity. Any smart restaurant owner knows exactly what their restrooms cost them to operate on a monthly basis.

The brilliant part of the marketing system was to place the scrub in the restrooms with a sign that read - Free hand massages on us - The scrub included a spoon and directions on how to use it. At the bottom of the sign it said - Available for purchase here -

A display of the scrubs was placed next to the cash register. When the customers were paying for their meal it was very easy to purchase a scrub at the same time. No competition, no other scrubs in the area and the plan worked brilliantly.

Within two days I had the scrub placed in seven different restaurants. Not one restaurant owner said no to the idea of making money from of his or her restrooms.

Never in my wildest dreams would I have ever came up with the scrub idea. Even more unlikely was the idea of how to market the scrub in restaurants. Nothing in my personal mental programming would have led me to think of such an idea. I soon became known as the "scrub guy" at work. I was selling them to my co-worker flight attendants.

It was my thought process of wanting to open a business that led me to ask my friend about a boat dealership.

Lack of money + desire to open a business + a conversation about a boat dealership with a friend and restaurant owner + his discovery of how to market scrubs in a restaurant = My own sea salt scrub business.

We called it Nature's Body Scrub. My cost was $3.98 for a 16 ounce jar, we sold each jar for $19.95

Change how you think. Start to read the books and watch for the opportunities around you. Collect information in any way you can. Google search, passive income ideas. When an opportunity arises you will recognize it because you have trained your brain to think differently. It is equally important to be in a position to take advantage of the opportunities when they come along.

"But I can't think of anything to do for passive income."

You are an expert at something. This doesn't mean you have a formal degree in that area of expertise. Here's how to figure out what that something is. I was taught this by one of my financial coaches.

Get a normal piece of paper and draw a line from top to bottom down the center of the paper. On the left side, write down everything your friends would tell others, that you are passionate about. If I ask your friends, what you are passionate about? What would they tell me about you? Write all those things down on the left side of the paper.

On the right side of the paper. Write down all the things you know a great deal about. For example my friends call me when they are looking to buy a motorcycle. Why do they call me? Because I have bought and sold motorcycles my whole life. I'm passionate about bikes and my friends know this about me. Do I have a degree in motorcycles? No, but if such a degree existed they would probably call me to teach the class. That's the kind of stuff you write down on the right side of the paper. Write down as many things as you can think of that you know a great deal about. Write down the kind of stuff your friends ask you about for advice. You may want to refer to your list of thirty things to do before you die.

Look at both sides of the paper and find the stuff on the left side your (passionate) side that matches up with stuff on the right side your (expertise) side. Connect the two sides that match with a line through the center of the paper. Do this with all items that match up. In the middle of the paper where the lines all cross each other is called your zone of expertise. This is where you start. You now have a platform for your book, podcast, blog, or cellphone app. Chose one and start working.

Destroying the Myths of Debt

"Yeah but, even if I wanted to start a business I don't have any money. It takes money to make money right?"

Usually the person who says this is the same person who just cut up a $10,000 credit card, and they wonder why they don't have any money.

Debt in my opinion is one of the most misunderstood concepts in the financial world, at least amongst the 90 percenters. The 90 percenters fear debt more than just about anything, many of them to the point of depression or suicide. How tragic to ruin the lives of countless human beings over a stupid piece of green paper that in reality has no real value at all.

Quite literally, the paper it's printed on isn't worth a few pennies. I found the following numbers on the federal reserve website. www.federalreserve.gov.

Cost to print paper money.
5.4 cents to print $1 and $2 dollar bills.
11.5 cents to print a $5 dollar bill
10.9 cents for the $20 dollar bill
19.4 cents for the $50 dollar bill.
15.5 cents to make a $100 dollar bill.

If you lend a friend or family member money, who's at risk, the lender or the borrower?

If I ask you for a $100,000 loan, and you lend it to me. Who is at risk? You are of course! You as the lender is the only one who stands to lose anything.

"Oh sorry, I can't pay the $100,000. What's that you say? You're going to ruin my credit score? Ahh shucks... have a great day! See ya!" says the borrower.

It's quite simple to see that the lender is the one at risk. Then why are you so afraid of debt and why do you believe that you as the borrower is at risk?

Is it because of some moral obligation? Or is it social programing by the industrialist? Perhaps a respected leader in the community taught you to fear debt. Maybe you're worried about some ethical obligation. Is that how the bank looks at it when they are taking a home away from a family, putting them out on the street? Or the widow woman whose husband left her with nothing. Did the bank give her a helping hand allowing her to stay in the home she raised her children in? Absolutely not! They gave her an eviction notice with a date to **get out!**

The banks are ruthless when it comes to getting their money back. Trust me, moral obligation is never in the terms of a bank's loan contracts. So why are you so morally bound to pay back that loan? Think about it, what is the worst thing that can happen if you can't pay back your loans?

Before you answer that question, I want you to really think about your answers. Do you know if what you're saying is true or, is what you are thinking something "THEY" would say?

Was your first thought something like *"bankruptcy stays on your record for 7 years,"* or *"you'll never get a loan again."* Are you sure these statements are true or did you just hear that from some unknown source?

If you borrow money to buy a home, and the bank later takes the home because you couldn't pay. You're no worse off than you were before you bought the home. You're in the same position you were before you borrowed the money. Only now you don't have a monthly payment to worry about. So why are you so afraid? If you think about it, it's likely your monthly payment was the thing causing you the most stress, even more than the thoughts of the overall loan itself.

Again why are you so afraid of debt? How much do you really know about debt? What is your ultimate goal in regards to debt? Do you cut up credit cards? Do you eat rice and beans, live miserably and go without to save a little extra money, and then use that money to pay down your debt? Who told you this was a smart way to handle debt? Can you pinpoint a time in your life when you learned this? Where did this belief come from? Is it truly the best way to get ahead financially?

Most of the millionaires I know have very large amounts of debt and six or seven credit cards in their wallet or purse. Why would they borrow money if they are millionaires?

Wouldn't they pay cash for everything? If cutting up credit cards and living a miserable life and giving every extra penny to the bank is the way to become rich, then why aren't the rich doing that same thing?

You don't see them eating cheap tv dinners and sending every penny they save to the bank so the banker can eat a fancy dinner, and why do they pay for dinner with a credit card?

Some so called financial experts tell you to cut up your credit cards. Yet they are flying first class to the next financial seminar where 30,000 people bought a ticket online using a credit card to hear them speak. They tell you to cut up your credit cards, but their entire business model is built around being able to charge your credit card online. Do you think they bought a first class ticket without a credit card?

Is what you believe about debt really true at all? Have you ever heard of good debt or is all debt bad? There is such a thing as good debt.

I first learned about good debt in Robert Kiyosaki's book - Rich Dad Poor Dad - in it he has a very simple definition.

"**Good debt** puts money in your pocket. **Bad debt** takes money out of your pocket."

90 percenters say they don't have any money to invest but they cut up a $10,000 credit card. 90 percenters say "It takes money to make money."

But you probably get several pre approved credit card offers in the mail everyday. What is a credit card? It's a piece of plastic linked to digital numbers in a computer. If you borrow $10,000 from the bank in the form of credit cards, who's at risk? It's the bank's money not yours.

It's true most of us feel some sort of ethical obligation, and maybe we should, but not to the point of being suicidal or continually stressed or afraid of financial collapse.

If you borrow money and can't pay it back what's the worst that can happen? Are they going to take away your birthday? You may lose the material possessions you bought with the money, if that happens you are no worse off than before you borrowed the money.

A credit card is money you can use to buy an asset with no collateral. If you default on the card you keep the asset.

"Yeah but, my credit score will be affected in a bad way."

And? Your point is? Why are you afraid of a credit score? Isn't your goal to get out of debt? What's the purpose of a credit score? It's to allow you to borrow more money!

If your goal is to get out of debt, why do you want a score that allows you to get deeper into debt?

Have you ever told someone you're waiting for your ship to come in? Well it's not coming because it has a great big hole in it called a credit score. You say your goal is to get out of debt but you go to great lengths to make sure you can borrow more money in the future. Good luck with that.

I am not in any way saying you should borrow money with the intent of never paying it back. Only by paying back the debt and keeping a good credit score can you borrow more money for future Investments through traditional loans. Your credit score is important because it says you are trustworthy and can live up to your end of a contract. Not just for banks but for private investors as well. I'm simply trying to open your eyes about the truth behind debt and who's at risk. It's not worth depression, suicide or ruining life's precious moments worrying about debt.

Remember, true wealth is time and the goal should be to generate more of it. Take a look at the following example about debt.

Let's say you make $3,000 a month at your Job. Let's also say you have a $10,000 debt with a minimum monthly payment of $200.

You eat rice and beans to save money so you can pay down your debt, you don't go out to dinner, you don't go to the movies, you stop doing all the fun stuff that makes life worth living just so you can make extra payments.

Or let's say you do all that stuff and you set the money aside until you have the full $10,000 all at once. That $10,000 is yours, it's in your possession it's money you have right now. If you use your $10,000 to pay off the debt you will never see that money again. It's gone forever.

If you use the $10,000 you saved to pay off the debt, did you increase your gross income of $3,000? No, your gross income is still $3,000. Did it create more time for you? No, but they say "Well, I have an extra $200." No you don't, you still gross $3,000 a month. You always had the $200 but you don't earn more than $3,000 a month by paying off the debt. You don't have extra just because you paid off the loan.

Yes, it's true you have less of a financial obligation by paying off a debt but it did not increase your gross income. You still gross $3,000 a month. If you want that $200 you still have to go to work. You didn't create more time by getting out of debt.

If your lifestyle requires $3,000 a month, and you pay off a debt using the $10,000 you saved by eating rice and beans. What happens if the day after you pay off the debt, you lose your job? You are out on the street with no money to pay your bills. If you still had the $10,000 you would have enough money to take just over three months looking for a new job or a better way to make money before you had to think about downsizing your lifestyle.

But I thought you didn't like risk?

By paying off the debt you opened yourself up to a new level of risk. You will never see that $10,000 again. How long is it going to take you to make another $10,000 for investing or savings if you use the money you saved by eating rice and beans to pay off the debt?

I'm not going to show you the math on how much you will lose by not investing the $10,000 and using it to pay off debt instead. Once you've paid the debt you have to go back to eating rice and beans for another 5 years to get another $10,000 before you can invest.

Why not take the $10,000 you already have and invest it in something that earns $200 a month instead of using it to get out of debt. Then use the $200 you earn from the investment to make the monthly payment on the debt.

Investment of $10,000 = $200 per month net income.

Use the net of $200 and pay the $200 loan payment. Instantaneously the relief on your earned income of $3,000 is the same as if you payed off the debt. You no longer have to take the money out of your paycheck for the loan payment.

The new asset you purchased with the $10,000 is making the payment for you. You are still living up to your contract with the lender, you're making your monthly payment, your credit score is not affected, it's still great.

Eventually your new asset will pay off the debt. What I'm saying is, instead of paying off the debt then waiting until you have another $10,000 to invest. Why not take the $10,000 you have from eating rice and beans and invest it right now? Then let it make the payment on your debt for you? Once the debt is paid off you will still have the $10,000 investment, and it's still making you $200 a month.

Again with the 90 percenter concerns… "Yeah but, what about all the interest I will pay over the term of the loan?"

The minute your new investment starts to make the payment on the loan you no longer pay interest.

I can see your wheels turning… stay with me. Interest is still being paid but not by you, it's no longer coming out of your paycheck. Your new investment is paying the interest. Once you have the asset that makes the loan payment for you, you personally never pay another dime in interest. It's not coming out of your personal paycheck, the asset pays it for you.

Once your new asset has paid off the loan balance you still have your $10,000 and it's still making $200 a month. Now you truly have an extra $200. Add it to your $3,000 paycheck and now you're making $3,200 a month. Now you can afford to take a day off, you just generated more time. You can take a day off from work because you only need $3,000 to maintain your current lifestyle.

If you really want to go crazy, you can continue to take $200 out of your gross income and pay on the debt along with the $200 from your new $10,000 investment and kill your debt in half the time. But why would you do that? Why not use the money to buy another $10,000 asset and make another $200 per month passive income?

Why not borrow $10,000 to buy an asset in the first place?

If I borrow $10,000 and I use it to buy something that makes $400 a month with a minimum payment of $200 a month.
I profit a $200 net gain every month above what the loan is costing me. I do not care what the interest rate is or if it's for 100 years, it's making me $200 per month more than it's costing me. I'm not the one paying the interest, my investment pays the interest. I never have to be afraid of Interest ever again.

Interest is the real reason the 90 percenters are afraid of debt. Mainly because they don't understand it.

They say "The interest will cost me a lot of money over the terms of the loan."

"How much is it going to cost you in dollars?" I ask.

"I don't know exactly, but it's a lot," says the 90 percenter.

"Do you know how to calculate the interest?"

"No," is the reply.

"Then how do you know it's going to cost you a lot?" I ask.

"Well (THEY) say it will cost me a lot." Is the only answer the 90 percenter can come up with.

If I use debt to buy an asset. I personally don't pay interest, the asset pays the interest. If I use debt to buy a liability then yes, I trade minutes of my life working to pay interest.

"Yeah but, if I just pay cash for everything I don't have to worry about interest at all."

True, but you do have to worry about losing everything. By paying cash you assume 100% of the risk and you are destroying your earning potential by not leveraging your money.

Who makes more money? The person who pays cash for an investment, or the person who finances the same investment?

Andrew and Brian receive $40,000 each as an inheritance. They find a group of homes under foreclosure listed for sale at $40,000 per home. Each home will rent for $650 per month.

Andrew decides to pay cash for one of the homes and starts to collect $650 per month in rent.

Brian decides to finance one of the homes using a traditional loan with a 20% down payment. Brian's loan is for 30 years with a 4.1% investment loan interest rate.

At the end of the 30 year loan period who will have made a better return on their investment (ROI) Andrew or Brian?

All it takes to find out is simple math, nothing complicated just simple addition, subtraction and division.

Andrew paid $40,000 cash and purchased one home. The rental income is $650. Before Andrew can call any of the rental income profit, he has to get his original investment of $40,000 back in his pocket.

To find out how long it will take to get his money back divide his original investment of $40,000 by the rental income of $650 simple right?

$40,000 ÷ $650 = 61.5384615385 month's

It will take Andrew just under 62 months to get his original investment of $40,000 back in his pocket.

30 years = 360 months

With the investment terms of 30 years minus the 62 months it will take to get his money back. Andrew has 298 months to earn a profit of $650 per month.

360 - 62 = 298 months

To find how much Andrew will net on his rental property over the 30 years. Multiply the rental income by the number of months he will make a profit.

$650 rent × 298 months = $193,700 net income over the 30 years.

To find Andrews percentage of return on investment or ROI. Divide his net income of $193,700 by the 30 years to find his net per year.

$193,000 ÷ 30 = $6456 net income per year.

Divide the annual income by the original investment amount of $40,000.

$6456 ÷ $40,000 = .1614

Move the decimal point to the right two spaces .1614 to 16.14 and you have the percentage of return. Andrew made a 16.14% return on his investment or ROI.

What about Brian who uses debt to buy his rental home?

Brian uses $8,000 of his original $40,000 as a downpayment on his rental home. He finances the remaining $32,000 at 4.1% interest over 30 years.

Brian's monthly payment is $154.62 He charges the same $650 for rent as Andrew.

$40,000 - $8,000 down = $32,000 loan or debt.

$32,000 financed at 4.1% for 30 years or 360 months.

Monthly payment is $154.62

Rental income $650 - $154.62 loan payment = $495.38 net income per month.

Before Brian can claim a profit from his rentals he - like Andrew - must get his original investment money back. Instead of $40,000, Brian only has $8,000 of his own money in the deal.

$8,000 ÷ rental profit of $495.38 = 16.149 month's

In just over 16 months Brian has his original investment of $8,000 back in his pocket. He has another 344 month's worth of rental income over the 30 year term.

344 months × $495.38 = $170,410.72 net income after 30 years.

Brian turned $8,000 into $170,410.72

To find Brian's return on investment take his net income and divide it by 30 years to find his annual net income of $5,680 per year.

$170,410.72 ÷ 30 yrs = $5,680 net income per year.

Divide Brian's annual net income of $5,680 by his original $8,000 out of pocket to find his percentage of return.

$5,680 net ÷ $8,000 investment = .71

Move the decimal point to the right two spaces to find Brian's 71% return on investment.

Andrew invested $40,000 with a 16% ROI.
Brian invested $8,000 with a 71% ROI.

Brian isn't finished, he financed one rental home with $8,000 of his own money. He still had $32,000 of his original $40,000 inheritance money in his pocket. He can do the same thing with 4 more homes. Brian buys 5 homes with five $8,000 down payments. He did this on day one of his 30 year investment. Each home will net him the same $170,410.72 after 30 years.

$170,410.72 × 5 homes = $852,053.6

Brian turns his $40,000 into $852,053.6 by leveraging his money using debt.

Andrew turns his $40,000 into $193,700 by paying cash.

Do you still think paying cash is the way to become wealthy?

3 of Brian's 5 rental homes could go empty and all of Brian's expenses will be covered by the 2 homes that are still rented.

16 months after Brian bought his 5th rental homes he has his original $40,000 investment money back in his pocket. He could buy another 5 homes doing the same thing all over again. What does Andrew have in his pocket after 16 months?

16 month's × $650 rental income = $10,400 that he is saving until he has another $40,000 so he can pay cash for his second home. He still isn't able to enjoy any extra profit for his investment. It's going to take him 62 months to get his original investment of $40,000 back in his pocket.

    At the same 16 month mark, Brian has 5 homes netting $495.38 per home per month for a total monthly income of $2,476.9 per month and he has his original $40,000 in his pocket.

    If Brian reinvests his $40,000 two more times in the same way. He will have 15 homes within 24 months and over **4.2 million dollars** worth of assets and net income in 32 years. (Assuming the home values go up 5% per year making them worth $100,000 over the 30 year term)

    In just over 32 years Brian is earning $9,750 per month in rental income. His loans are paid in full and he no longer has a monthly payment on any of them.

Andrew will have 3 homes and $881,100 in assets and net worth and is earning $1,950 per month in rental income.

At the end of the 30 years.
Brian has,
15 homes debt free
$9,750 net rental income per month.
$117,000 per year
$4.2 million in total assets and net income.

Andrew has,
3 homes debt free
$1,950 net rental income per month.
$23,400 per year
$881,100 total assets and net income over the same 30 years.

How much interest did Brian pay on his 15 rental homes over the past 30 years? Zero, zip, nada!

Brian didn't pay one dime of interest. His renters paid 100% of the loan interest while Brain made $495.3 positive cash flow every month per home. Two drastically different outcomes with the same $40,000 possibility.

This is a very simplified example of rental properties. Actual rentals require additional consideration for other expenses. I've simplified it to show the power of leveraging your money through debt.

Savings

What about your savings account is it an asset or a liability?

Is saving money really doing you any good? If you haven't figured it out by now I'm probably going to destroy your warm fuzzy feeling about your savings account. At this point, how much of what you thought you knew about money was wrong?

You've probably been told your entire life to save money, but have you ever done the math to see if it's really a smart thing to do?

"What math?" You ask.

Well, calculating the loss of purchasing power due to inflation of the dollar. Your money is losing value at a faster rate than any other time in history because of inflation, caused by manipulation of markets and the printing of more money. Printing more money causes your exciting money to go down in value. The more money they print the less the existing bills are worth.

If you have $10,000 in the bank congratulations, you have more than most people and I'm sure you feel all warm and fuzzy about it. But did you know In 2007 a 25 lb bucket of wheat was $8. One year later the same bucket of wheat was

$14. In 2007 your $10,000 would have bought 1250 buckets of wheat. Just one year later at $14 per bucket the same $10,000 savings can only buy 714 buckets of wheat. You lost 43% of your purchasing power. You lost money by saving it.

My grandfather told me of a time when he paid $1 per acre for land. Yes you read it right $1 for an acre of land. When I tell people this their reaction is always the same. "Yeah but, that was back then."

Let's put it into perspective, $1 was equal to one day's worth of work. At the same time my grandfather was paying $1 per acre of land, he was making $1 per day for his labor. With one day's worth of wages he could buy an acre of land. How many acres of land can you buy today with one day's worth of work?

As I'm writing this book, in the Salt Lake City area 1 acre of land is well over $100,000. I don't know anyone that works 9 to 5 that is making $100,000 per day.

The value of land did not go up! The value of the dollar went down. In my grandfather's day the dollar had the value of an acre of land or the value of a day's worth of Labor. Today a dollar doesn't have the value of a cup of coffee. It takes 100 thousand $1 bills to equal the value of an acre of land.

I'm sure if you would have told my grandfather that one day land would cost $100,000 per acre, he would have laughed at you and called you crazy.

The green paper dollar bill is losing value daily at a faster rate than ever before. In 2010 the U.S. mint was printing 1 billion dollars per day.

Prior to 1971 The Federal Reserve was required to have $1 worth of gold for every dollar that was printed. In 1971 president Nixon, without the approval of Congress released the gold standard allowing any number of bills to be printed without gold to back it up. Since that day the dollar has continued to lose value faster than ever before.

In the early 1900s a $20 gold coin was minted. It was one ounce of gold. It had the same value as a $20 bill. In 1903 the $20 bill and the $20 gold coin would both buy you the same amount of stuff.

In the 1900's a hotdog at a baseball game would cost you around 3 cents and a beer was 2 cents. With $20, gold or paper you could buy 666 hotdogs or 1000 beers. Put the gold coin and the $20 bill in a shoebox in 1903 and hide them until today.

According to money.CNN the $20 bill in 2017 will buy you 3 beers and 5 hot dogs at a baseball game. The $20 gold piece however will buy you 330 hotdogs plus 198 beers to wash them down. You better be hungry and I recommend you find a good AA group before you start drinking the beers.

It's not that the gold will make you rich, drunk maybe but not rich. It just holds its value when the green paper dollar bill does not. The price of gold and silver fluctuates daily with its ups and downs but with a steady upward climb over time. 1 oz of gold was worth $20.67 in the year 1900. Today the same ounce of gold is worth $1,400 not including rare coin values.

The green dollar bill has fluctuated also but with a rapid decline over time. In the year 1900 a $1 bill had the value of an acre of land. Today the $1 bill will buy you a small bite of a hotdog and you will need 99,999 more $1 bills to buy an acre of land.

By sitting on your green dollar bills and calling it a savings you are losing money every day.

The key here is to save something that holds value or goes up in value. Assets... save assets, things that make you money or go up in value over time. It can be any number of things. Gold and silver are a couple examples.

I personally save silver, mainly for the ease of selling it during hard times. With 1 oz of gold you will need to find a buyer that can afford to pay you the $1,400 for that piece of gold. In an emergency situation, if you need a gallon of milk and all you have is 1 oz of gold, guess what you're paying for that milk? But if you have a roll of silver dimes that are worth a $1.50 each, you can easily barter or trade a few dimes for that gallon of milk.

Silver is easy to buy. All of my kids have a silver savings jar. I tell them to put something of everything they make in the jar.

"I don't care how much it is, just put something of every dollar you make in the jar." I tell them.

When I get ready to buy silver I ask them "who has silver money?"

I take their money along with my own and I purchase silver. It was fun to watch, it became a kind of competition amongst the kids to see who owned the most silver.

You may not have $1,400 dollars to buy a one ounce gold coin, but you can skip a soda one day and buy a silver dime or spend $20 on a 1 oz silver round. If you do this once a week you'll be shocked at how fast your little treasure chest of silver will grow.

I highly recommend keeping a certain amount of cash on hand for emergencies. A good rule of thumb is about three months worth of expenses in cash.

So why is understanding inflation important?

Let's use your home loan as an example. You eat rice and beans and work extra hours to make extra payments on your home loan. Let's do the math to see if it's worth it.

A typical home Loan in 2017 would range from $180,000 to $350,000 at 3.2 to 4.1 percent interest rate over 30 years.

No investor would call this a good deal?

Would you lend someone $250,000 to make 3.8 percent over 30 years? Who would say, "I'm going to lend you $250,000 for 30 years to only make 3.8% return on my money?" This is a terrible deal no investor in their right mind would ever go for it.

So why do the banks do it? The number one reason the bank sees this as a good deal is because they know most borrowers think like a 90 percenter. Based on years of dealing with 90 percenters, they know 90 percenters won't keep the original loan for 30 years. 90 percenters typically refinance every 5 to 7 years.

Note: *Most of the interest is accrued in the first 5 years.*

The banker also knows 90 percenters are going to make extra payments on the loan. Do you realize that by making extra payments you don't reduce your risk but you reduce the bank's risk?

If you're paying more per month than the loan contract calls for, you put more money in the bankers pocket and less in yours. The banker now has less money in the deal and if you default on the loan, the banker still gets all your stuff.

If you have a $100,000 home loan and you eat rice and beans and live a miserable life going without, you don't go to the movies or out to dinner or to the ball game. You give up all the things that make life worth living and you managed to pay off $99,000 of that debt.

What happens if you get in a terribly bad accident and are no longer able to physically work for money? As a result you can't pay the remaining $1,000 of the debt, what happens to your home?

The bank takes it from you! (along with the $99,000 you already paid them.)

Every miserable moment you put yourself through trying to earn extra money to make extra payment was all for nothing. You missed out on life's precious moments that you will never get back.

What was the banker doing that entire time? Eating steak dinner with his girlfriend and taking her to the ballgame, then spending a night in the Ritz-Carlton after the Super Bowl using your money. Yep, the very money you traded life's most valuable minutes for just so you could make extra payments because of your fear of interest.

You entered into a contract. You said you were going to take 30 years to pay it back, why not just stick with the contract? If you said because of the interest. Then let me ask you this… how much interest are you going to pay in dollars? Do you even know how to calculate the amount in dollars? Where did your current belief about interest come from? "Well they say" is the interest really costing you as much as you think it is?

90 percenters are afraid of interest but they don't know how to calculate it. It's human nature to be afraid of things we don't understand.

Let's go back to the $8 bucket of wheat. The reason the bank wants you to make extra payments is because it's in today's value of money. If you pay an extra $200 payment per month, the bank can reinvest that $200 in today's value. (they can buy 30 beers and 50 hotdogs with that $200 today) How much is that $200 going to be worth 30 years from now? I wouldn't be surprised if you can't buy a cup of coffee for $200 in 30 years at the rate we are going. If you think I'm crazy just remember what I said about telling my grandfather that the land he paid $1 for would someday cost $100,000.

The point is, inflation will offset the interest you will pay on your home loan. If your monthly payment is $1,000 today how much is your monthly payment 28 years from now on a 30-year loan? It's still $1,000.

$1,000 twenty eight years from now isn't going to buy much. The current rate of inflation will offset the interest you paid at the beginning of the loan. Again by making extra payments you alleviate the risk on the banks part not yours.

Let's do a little more math. How much money do you lose by making extra payments instead of investing. Let's use $200 for the amount. You could buy eight gumball machines at $25 each. If those 8 machines average $20 a month. You will make an extra $160 per month, or $1,920 dollars per year.

Over the term of your loan that $200 would make you $57,600. By making an extra $200 per month payment you lost $57,600 per $200 spent over the term of the loan. If you buy 8 new machines every month for thirty years you will have a total of 2880 machines.

2880 x $20 per month equals $57,600 per month or $691,200 per year.

You lost enough money to pay for your home almost seven times. You're better off sticking with the terms of the contract.

Why do we refinance every 5 to 7 years?

Because the bank is going to make you an offer in five years to get you to refinance. It will cost you $2,600 in closing cost to reduce your monthly payment by $50 per month and reset your loan for another 30 years. This is where they coined the phrase "laughing all the way to the bank."
Making extra payments on your loan definitely cuts down on the interest paid and shortens the length of the loan significantly. The pay down the loan method does work, but in the end you haven't built any true wealth. You may own your home outright but it's not making you any money. You still have expenses. You have property tax and maintenance, utilities,

hoa fees and the upkeep on the landscaping just to mention a few. Is your debt free home putting money in your pocket or taking it out of it?

It's taking money out of your pocket every month. Remember, liabilities take money out of your pocket.

"Yeah but, I have the equity in my home."

What is equity?

Equity is a speculated value you believe someone will pay you for your home if you sold it. Try turning it into cash in an emergency. If something happens and you need cash tomorrow, good luck using the equity in your home. Even a home equity line of credit takes a few days to set up in most cases. What is the equity doing to make you money? How much income are you losing by not investing that money? Invest the money and let it make the payment on your home.

I find it interesting that the 90 percenters will make the 20% down payment on their home and then shortly thereafter will take out a second mortgage with the same bank and make them two payments with interest.

It's a brilliant plan by the banker if you think about it.

They will lend you enough money to buy a home if you give them 20% down. 6 months later they will lend you 20% of the value of your home with interest. They simply turn around and lend you your own money and they charge you for it. Again, laughing all the way to the bank. Yet the 90 percenters continually do this over and over again because hey, that's what everyone does right? Remember the Vegas crowd?

90 percenters believe they have less risk with a debt free home. Even owning your home debt free, you still have expenses like property tax. If you can't physically work and as a result you can't pay your taxes you can still lose your home. Your local county court house holds regular auctions selling homes and land for delinquent taxes. You also open yourself up to the chance of a lawsuit if someone gets hurt on your property and decides to sue, they will go after the equity in your home. If your home is maxed out in debt, they don't have any equity to sue you for. Case dismissed.

I don't want you to get all worked up about the numbers and whether or not you should pay off your house. At this point you should continue doing what you are doing until you gain the financial education necessary to make the right decision for you and your current financial situation. This isn't intended to be an in depth education of how to invest or get out of debt. DON'T TRY AND FLY THE AIRPLANE WITHOUT INSTRUCTION! I'm simply pointing out small truths to change how you think about money. I also want you to think about your current financial programming, where did it come from and why do you think the way you do in regards to money?

I suspect that most of what you are reading isn't anything new. I'm just showing it to you in a different light. Hopefully helping you see things differently.

For most 90 percenters their mental wiring or mental programming is all that's keeping them from moving forward financially. The old ingrained belief system makes it nearly impossible to accept new things. When asked why they do what they do, they simply say because that's the way it's always been done. We don't want to ask questions or do the math or go against the crowd.

Time to change how we think. It's time to wake up and smell the cash flow. Is everything we think we know about money wrong? Everything we've been taught about money was designed to keep us in the workforce for at least 30 years and make the business owners filthy rich.

The good news is, there are no barricades keeping us from jumping over to the rich side of the fence. There are no laws keeping you and I from becoming wealthy. The only thing holding us back is our financial programming. Where did your current financial beliefs come from?

I hope by now you're starting to see that it's your current financial mindset that is holding you back. Your limitations are in your own mind and therefore can be controlled and changed by you. You don't have chains tied to your feet keeping from achieving financial success. The only true limiting factor is your own mind. Granted your circumstances will play a part in how long it may take you to create your financial future but ultimately you are in control. **P+R=O**

Changing how you think about money inevitably affects your financial future. Like it or not your future has already been altered due to the fact that you are reading this book. The next time you are faced with a financial decision you will think and react differently than you would if you had not discovered this book. Sometimes that small change in your thought process is the difference between $10 and $1 million dollars in the future.

You didn't find this book by accident, something in your current thought process caused you to start reading it. Call it luck or ovarian lottery, either way you have changed your financial future in ways you can not yet see.

Knowing isn't Good Enough, You Have to Act.

I was invited to hear a friend of mine speak at a financial seminar. A few days after his seminar I was telling him how much I enjoyed it. I was surprised to hear him say he doesn't like doing seminars. When I asked why, he said it was for a couple of reasons.

He said, "Only about 1% of the audience ever listens to any speaker."

He also said most people can't relate to him when he starts throwing around the "b word" a billion dollars. People tend to shut down and instantly feel like they are listening to something that has no value for them. It seems unrealistic.

As I thought about this he was absolutely right. During the next several seminars I attended I observed the audience closely. It was easy to see who was interested and who was not. I also found, it was hard to relate to people that speak about making several million dollars from just one of their ideas or investments. It seems to unrealistic or out of reach for the average person. We never truly believe that we could be as successful as they are. So why are we wasting time sitting in the seminar in the first place if we aren't going to do something with the information they are sharing?

I know I will never be as wealthy as Warren Buffett or Bill Gates but that doesn't mean I can't learn from them. It's too easy to give up before we even get started. We get discouraged at the thought of never being able to reach the level of wealth as the billionaires.

We need to change our mindset and realize that becoming a master of our time and money is a must no matter how large or small the amount.

It may come as a surprise, but you may be closer to true wealth than a friend or neighbor of yours who is making double what you are making right now.

If your friend is making $10,000 a month, it's a fairly safe bet to say they need at least $10,000 per month to maintain their current lifestyle. If they lose their job they will have to change the lifestyle within two weeks. In order for your friend to be truly wealth and not change their lifestyle they will need to find enough passive income assets to generate $10,000 per month.

If you are making half what your friend is making, $5,000 per month, you only need to find passive income assets that make $5,000 instead of $10,000 before you are truly free having both time and money.

So don't get discouraged when you hear stories of the rich and famous. They are not you. You have your own story to create and your own levels of wealth to obtain. Focus on you and only you. Take what you learn from the rich and use only what applies to your current situation. Don't go to a financial seminar by Warren Buffet thinking you will learn something that will make you as rich as he is. Just go with the intent to better your personal financial situation. Look for the information that will help you take the next step towards true freedom and don't compare yourself to them. A great way to keep from getting discouraged when you listen to them speak is to have your plan already laid out and know where you want to go before you start attending the seminars.

Willpower

In the book called - *How to Fail at Almost Everything and Still Win Big - by Scott Adams*, he talks about "willpower."

Scott says, "if something requires willpower it's not sustainable."

I believe this to be true. Have you ever started a goal or set a New Year's resolution only to quit within the first couple of weeks? Well you're not alone.

We thought willpower was going to see us through. Willpower requires a great amount of energy and discipline, it's nearly impossible to carry on for any length of time.

According to Forbes.com about 40% of Americans set New Year's resolution but only 8% keep them.

Many New Year's resolutions require willpower to keep going. However, I did find - with the help of Scott's book - that once you create a system, willpower is no longer needed.

I have a fitness gym in the basement of my home. My goal was to workout for 1 hour everyday. But that would require willpower that I didn't have to walk downstairs to the gym. The thoughts of an hour long workout had me exhausted before I even started. The thought alone was destroying any motivation. I didn't like spending an hour in the gym but I would waste two hours watching TV. How lazy is it to have a gym in my home and I couldn't get motivated to walk down the stairs?

One day I thought about bringing a few weights into the TV room. I grabbed a couple of 25 pound weights and an exercise ball. I took them upstairs and placed them in front of the TV.

Every time there was a commercial I would start to exercise. I didn't have a set time to workout or a weight limit. I would simply do something every time a commercial interrupted the show I was watching. I just did something, that's it. No time limit, no specific exercise, I just did something during every commercial. Much to my surprise, after a few days my energy level went up. I found myself craving the workout. I was actually looking forward to the commercials.

As the days went by my strength increased and the desire to workout became stronger. I soon moved into the basement where I began a full exercise routine and willpower was no longer required. The driving force was an addiction to working out. It took willpower to get started but the consistency of doing something everyday was the key to increase my strength and desire that motivated me to keep going.

Since I didn't have a time limiting goal I was mentally driven and inspired by positive thinking. By doing something everyday I wasn't disappointing myself by being upset when I didn't do a full hour.

Willpower alone will not sustain you. It's far better to create systems instead of goals. A system is doing something everyday forever. A goal has an end. Typically once you reach your goal you stop doing the things you were doing to achieve the goal. If your goals was to lose 5 pounds, you changed your diet and started working out. Once you reached the goal you stopped eating healthy and gave up the workout. Within a week you had already started to gain weight.

With a system to lose weight you might say something like, "I'm going to drink one less soda per day, or I'm going to take the stairs instead the escalator."

No goal with numbers of how many times you're going to take the stairs you just take the stairs every time from now on. Soon you have lost five pounds as a result of your new system and you will keep losing weight.

Scott covers goals and systems in great detail in his book. I highly recommend reading it. The same systems can be used when it comes to your time and money.

The Success Pyramid

Now that you know the P + R = O formula don't get caught in the trap of chasing the dollar. True freedom and happiness requires a well thought out plan along with a time budget that includes business, family, and beliefs. Your plan should start with a success pyramid.

To build your success pyramid you will need to start with a strong "WHY."

Why are you setting the goal in the first place? One reason people fall short of their dream is they don't have a strong enough why. You may want to spend some time thinking about your why and writing it down.

Another reason people fall short of their dreams is because they don't have a clear picture of where they want to go. Many people set goals but few know how to achieve them.

I'm sure you have at one time or another cut out a picture of something you wanted and stuck it on the fridge or maybe you wrote it on a 3 x 5 card and stuck it on your bathroom mirror. If so, good for you but how many times have you written down the steps required to accomplish that goal?

Having a goal without a plan or steps to follow for obtaining that goal, well that's like trying to build the roof of a house first without blueprints and no foundation or walls to start with.

The goal is something you build up to, it is the finished product. It's important to know where you want to end up.

If you call an airline and say I want to buy a ticket, the first question they are going to ask you is, "Where would you like to go?"

If you don't know the answer they won't be able to sell you a ticket. Once you have decided where you want to go, the next question is, "Where are you now?"

After you decide where you want to go, and you have decide where you are starting from, now you can build a plan to get you from where you are to where you want to be.

To build your success pyramid you need to start with your three W's.

WHY, WHAT and WHEN.

"**Why**" do you want the goal?
"**What**" is it going to take to get it?
"**When**" do you want it to happen?

Ultimate goal? I want to have enough passive income to quit my job.
Why? To spend more time with my family and never miss a birthday again.

What? What top three things must happen to accomplish my goal?
When? When do I want to quit my job? Within 5 years.

      Draw a box at the top of a piece of paper. Draw three boxes under that box. Draw three more boxes under each of those three boxes. Make them large enough to write severals lines in each box. When you're finished you should have something that looks like a pyramid. In the top box write the main goal, then write your "WHY" under the main goal in the same box. Your "WHY" is the most critical part of your goal. You must have a strong "WHY." If you don't, it's likely you won't make it very far. Without a strong "WHY" you won't put in the time and effort required to obtain your ultimate goal.

      You read about my "why" in chapter one. I wanted to find a better way to generate passive income to be able to spend more time with my family and be home for holidays and birthdays.

      You will need to dig deep and determine what your "why" is and make sure it is a strong one. You will need it to be strong enough to find motivation at times when things don't go as planned. Your "why" will help you to keep moving forward when times get tough. Your "why" should be aligned with your life's purpose.

      Next, in the same box write down the top three things that must happen in order to achieve your goal. These should be the top three things that when they are done your goal will happen no matter what. Still in the same box write down when you want your goal to happen be specific with a date and time.

Write down when you want each of the three parts of your goal to be completed. Do the same with all remaining boxes. Write the top three things that must happen to accomplish each level of your goal. In the next block or box of your pyramid write down the top three things that must happen to move to the next step of your goal and so on.

When you are finished, you will have a blueprint with your personal steps to success. You can actually see what is required to achieve your goal. If you do each small thing the goal will happen. Just like building a home if you start with the foundation and build it according to the blueprint you end up with the home you had planned for.

A great deal of what wealthy people have to teach us does apply and work for the average person. The secret is learning how to put what we learn into action. In other words we need to learn how to discipline ourselves to do what we already know we should be doing.

It's too easy to make excuses when we don't feel like doing what we should. It won't matter how many seminars we attend or the number of books we read if we don't do anything with the information we receive. It's one thing to know the secret behind the magic trick of making money. The real trick is doing something about it and putting into practice what you've learned. I have heard many excuses over the years as to why people don't do what they know they should be doing when it comes to money.

By far the number one excuse is " I don't have time."
I don't have time to start a business or read ten books about finances.

Masters of Time

A critical part of becoming wealthy is learning to master your time.

Typically at any given moment we already know we should be doing something else. We just don't care enough to make the change. It's easier to just get by than it is to come up with a plan to better our situation. It's even harder to put our plan into action. It's easier to set the cruise control on life and end up wherever the winds may take us. If you want a better life you will need to stand up take control and start moving forward.

One of my mentors taught me to develop a time budget not a time schedule, but a time budget. There is a difference. A schedule is what you do on a routine basis with no real goal in mind.

Example: get up in the morning, drive to work, work all day, drive home, watch tv, go to bed.

A time budget has a specific purpose for each hour of your time, with a specific objective or goal in mind.

Example: Spend one hour from 7:30pm to 8:30pm reading a book about passive income instead of spending the time on facebook.

Much like a financial budget, if you stick to it, you may find you have extra money at the end of the month. With a time budget I think you will be surprised at just how much time you really have.

    You will need to find a way to track your time. A simple planner or any timesheet will do as long as it has hourly time slots you can write in. You can find several types of daily planners with a simple google search.

    You're going to need two copies. On the first copy keep track of everything you do every hour of every day for the next seven days. If you sleep from 10:00pm to 7:00am write down slept in that section. If you work from 9 to 5 with a half hour lunch break. Write, worked from 9:00am to 12:00pm ate lunch from 12:00pm to 12:30pm then worked for 12:30pm to 5:00pm. If it takes you a half hour to drive home, write that down. If you watch tv for two hours write, watched tv in that section. If you take a nap write that down also. I'm sure you get the idea

    At the end of the week take a look at the time sheet and find the activities that you can't change like work, or commuting to work. Now transfer those activities to your new timesheet leaving out things with no objective or goal, like watching tv or spending time on facebook.

    Once you have transferred the important things take a look at all the empty spaces on the new timesheet. If you're anything like I was, you will discover that claiming I didn't have time wasn't true at all. Looking at your second time sheet with all the empty space is your new wake-up call. You're not looking at anything you didn't already know. The spaces in the new schedule are there to nudge you out of your comfort zone.

In the empty spaces on the new time sheet write down the things that are going to help you generate passive income and more free time in the future. The first things you write down should come from your success pyramid. Focus on finding time slots that allow you to do something every day towards your ultimate goal.

Some days may be harder than others. Monday you may have an extra three hours but on Tuesday you only have five minutes. That's ok just make sure you do something every day with the time you do have. Write things like read a new book, or attend a financial seminar or listen to a financial podcast. Write down the things you can do in those time slots that will help you get closer to the goals you have written down in your success pyramid.

Once you have them written in your schedule **do not change them.** These are known as the stones in your schedule. You can not move them. If you wrote down read a financial book from 7:00pm to 7:30pm you stick with it.

If your friends call and say "let's go to the movie at 7:00." you say, "I'm sorry I can't I have an appointment but I can go at 7:30."

If you don't budget your time for a specific objectives, there will always be something that will distract you from doing the things that are truly important for your financial future. Budget your time until it becomes a habit.

Be aware of wealth killers. What are wealth killers? Facebook, Twitter, YouTube, TV just to list a few.

For some people looking at Facebook posts from so called friends is more important than personal facetime, like a real face to face conversation with a real human being. You're not doing anything that will help you achieve success by wasting time on these types of wealth killers.

Much like all technology these things can give your business or personal goals a real boost when used correctly. 62% of marketers spend 6 hours a week on social media sites. 17% of them spend 20 hours a week. The average consumer spends an average of 3 hours a day or 21 hours a week on social media sites. Ask yourself, how much could you accomplish with an extra 20 hours a week working towards your business or personal goals.

Masters of Money

It doesn't take millions of dollars to become a master of them, in fact I know millionaires that are not masters of money.

The following information is around 8000 years old it has been repeated by many financial geniuses over the years and as far as I can tell it comes from the ancient city of Babylon.

When archaeologists uncovered the ruins of Babylon they found libraries of ceramic tablets. The tablets contain some of the earliest recordings of deeds to property and mortgage notes. I saw photos of one of theses tablets and I also read the translation. It was about a gentleman who had borrowed 38 1/16 shekels of silver. (1 shekel is equal to about .35 oz of silver.) It talked about the interest he would pay and was signed by five witnesses. It was dated 1823 BC.

I first read about these tablets in the book - *The Richest Man In Babylon* - by George S. Clason - I'm still not sure if the stories in his book are true or just based on information and lesson from the Babylonian tablets, but the principles contained in the book are solid and if you follow them they will transform you into a true master of money. I'm convinced our current modern day banking system is based on information found in those tablets.

It was not uncommon in the city of Babylon for people to put themselves or one of their family members up as collateral for a loan. Yes they did buy on credit back then. This meant that if you defaulted on your loan payments you would now become a literal slave to the person who lent you the money. If you could not live up to the terms of your loan contract you could be sold to another master. Imagine that, becoming a slave because of your debts.

I could go on and on about the lessons in Clason's book but I'm going to give you what I believe is the first step to becoming a master of money.

How much would you pay to go to lunch with a billionaire like Warren Buffet or Robert Kiyosaki, Steve Jobs or Napoleon Hill? A lunch with Warren Buffett sold at a charity auction for $3.5 million would you pay $20 for thirty minutes of his time? I would, but you don't have to. You can buy their books for around $15, almost every 10 percenter has written a book or someone has written a book about them, telling you and I exactly how they got where they are.

In the information age the only thing stopping us from achieving true freedom and happiness in life is how we react to the possibilities found in the information we can learn from everyone that has gone before us, as far back as 8000 years ago.

My favorite part in Clason's book is when a gentleman named Dabesir goes to visit the gold lender Mathon. Mathon starts to make fun of Dabesir thinking he is there to borrow money.

"Did a woman take your money Dabasire?" he laughs.

"No, I've come to ask you how you make your gold," says Dabesir, catching Mathon off guard.

Mathon repliers "In all my years as a gold lender, and of all the hundreds of people that have visited me to borrow gold, not one has ever asked me how I make my gold."

Mathon is impressed by Dabesir's request and invites him to dine with him as he explains how he makes his gold.

You can learn to master your money on any income level or any budget. In order to master your money or become a master of it, you will need to learn the first rule of gold that Mathon taught Dabesir.

Clason's Book - The Richest Man in Babylon - calls this "getting your purse to fatten."

The first rule of gold: *"A portion of all you earn is yours to keep."* In other words pay yourself first.

You've probably heard this most of your life. What does it mean to pay yourself first? Why pay yourself first and not last or in the middle of the month somewhere? Simple answer ""pain" yep pain, not the physical kind of pain you feel when someone kicks you in the crockpot, but the kind of mental pain you put yourself through when you can't pay a bill on time. Pain, is the mother of creativity.

Why pay yourself first? If you pay yourself first, then at the end of the month you can't afford to pay the power bill, the power company is going to threaten to turn off your power. If you're like me this gets you out of your comfort zone and you start to feel some pain. It took me twenty years to realize pain is a good thing. Pain is the mother of creativity. It's going to force you to find a way to pay the power bill.

With the threat of pain the creative side of your mind that has been sleeping is now wide awake and trying to find a way to pay the power bill. You never go back to the money you used to pay yourself first. If you pay the power bill first and at the end of the month you don't have enough money to pay yourself, there's no pain and the creative part of your brain stays asleep.

Pay yourself first... to do this right, you need to divide your money into four groups or categories. Each category is dedicated to a specific purpose, you will need to split it into percentages.

70 - 10 - 10 -10

70% Is for your Lifestyle account
10% Is for your Emergency account
10% Is for your Investing account
10% Is for your Charity account

Before we go any further…Don't worry if you can't do this right away, most people can't. I am going to show you how to get started on any financial budget.

The first category is where you pay yourself first and 10% is the goal. This is called your **Emergency account**. It's for emergencies only! You do not use this money for anything other than a major emergency. A new refrigerator isn't an emergency. Buying food because you lost your job and it's been a few weeks, ok maybe you could use some of this money for that.

70% percent of your income goes in your second category. This category is your **Lifestyle account**.

When dividing your money I found it's best to let your bank take care of as many of these accounts as possible. Most banks can do an automatic transfer every time your paycheck is deposited into your account.

I don't recommend the envelope and cash method where you label envelopes for each category and place the percentage of your cash in each one. Trying to hold onto cash is like trying to hold a handful of dry sand. Everytime you move your hand sand falls out. The more you try to protect it the more sand is lost. My wife and I tried this method and failed miserably. The first three months went great. I would ask my wife how we were doing and she would say great. Six months later I asked how much was in each envelope.

"Nothing," was her reply.

You can imagine my frustration.

"What happened to the money?" I asked.

"Hey Mom, I need lunch money today," says one of the kids.

In a rush to get everyone to school on time, the money was taken from the savings envelopes with the thought of *"I'll put it back later."* "Later" never comes. Cash is too easy to spend. I have my bank take care of two categories automatically. My 70% category and my 10% emergency category. I personally handle the other two.

The goal here is for 70% of your income to cover all of your expenses like, your house, your car, groceries, movie night and all of your wants. 70% of your income should cover 100% of your expenses. Everything you own and the monthly payments you owe should never cost more than 70% of your monthly income.

You're always going to have wants, even wealthy people want more stuff for some reason. Make a list of your wants and find the ones that fit in the 70% percent category then scratch off the rest. Again this is the goal, stick with me and I'll show the steps for reaching the goal of 70%.

The third category will contain another 10% of your income this is your **Investing account**. The purpose of this account is to help you eliminate emotion, you need to get rid of emotion when it comes to investing and use logic, reason and simple math. If you invest in something and you lose all your money, it doesn't matter, that's what it was for. You did your homework, you got the specialized education, you hired a mentor and for some unknown reason you still lost your money. Oh well, that's what is was for. It came out of your investment category. If you are afraid to lose money, you may miss out on the best deal of your life because you were afraid of losing a few bucks.

Losing the money from your investment account didn't affect your lifestyle because you have the 70% category that covers all your needs and wants and you still have your emergency fund of 10%. Losing the money in your investing account isn't going to put your family in a bind. But the fear of losing it could cost you a small fortune in lost investment potential.

Your friends says "I have a great idea for a business and I'll let you in on it for $300. We are going to bottle water and sell it for more per gallon than gasoline."

You say, "that's the dumbest idea I've ever heard, no-one will pay for water, it's free."

A one liter of water cost $2.65 per bottle. It takes just under 4 bottlers to equal a gallon.

$2.65 X 4 = $10.60 per gallon for water.
Gasoline is $2.54 per gallon.

You missed out on a billion dollar industry because you were afraid of losing $300 on the dumbest idea you've ever heard of.

The fourth category is also 10% and this one is your **Charity account**. The emotion caused by charity can destroy you financially even more so than the investing category if not kept under control.

How much should you give when you find someone in need? Let's say a family member has lost their job and is asking you for financial help. How much do you give them? This is the magic question and if you haven't thought about it beforehand you're in for a real struggle emotionally. Your heart tells you to give a very generous amounts, sometimes more than you can afford.

If all you have is a $20 bill and you give the family member the $20 to buy food, they eat for the day but what about you? You don't have enough money to buy a meal for yourself.

This was a very noble thing you did but now you're hungry, tired, and don't have energy as a result of not eating. You end up sick. You can't go to work and make more money. The family member returns and asks for your help. This time you have to tell them no, because you don't have any money. By giving more than you could afford, you put both of you in a bad spot, now neither one of you can eat.

You have to eliminate emotion when it comes to investing. The same is true when it comes to charity. You do this by setting aside 10% for just that, charity. When the family member asks you for help you can say yes let me check my account to see how much I have available. If you have $300 you can give it to them knowing it will not affect your personal budget. It didn't come from your 70% category and you still have your emergency and investment funds. You can tell them to come back next month and you will have another $300 for them. If you overdo charity it can damage your ability to earn more and in turn your ability to help in the future. Setting aside 10% gets rid of the emotion of charity saving you, and everyone you will help in the future from financial failure.

    I recently heard about a very wealthy man who is broke after making millions as a famous football quarterback. He was featured on one of those tv shows that talks about famous people who have lost everything.

    I felt terrible when I heard his story, I knew the man personally. I had been his pilot several times in a chartered private learjet. He was very generous and a kind, he was nice to everyone he spoke with and he would always give a very generous tip.

    So why was he broke? He overdid the charity category. He was too nice. He was paying for 96 cell phones. He paid for his home, Mom and Dad's home, the in-laws home and countless other charity type donations. It was only a matter of time before the money ran out. Now he has lost everything because he was too nice and didn't have a dedicated charity account.

Bill Gates and Warren Buffett give half of their net worth to philanthropy. I watched an interview with Warren Buffett where he said he calls every billionaire he knows and asks them to give up half of their net worth to charity. He said he gets told no sometimes. He also said he's going to write a book on how to get by on $500 million because apparently it's pretty hard to do.

There is a limit to charity and until we're making the kind of money that Bill and Warren are making, it's 10% percent.

70,10,10,10 is the 8000 year old formula for becoming a true master of money. For me personally this is one of the hardest things I ever did, and even still some months are harder than others.

Get Started at Any Income Level

I learned this trick from Robert Kiyosaki. Start with your three categories that require 10% percent. **Emergency - Investing - and Charity** put $1 per day in each category then adjust your lifestyle accordingly. You will find it doesn't take much of an adjustment to accommodate $1 per day. That's less than a 32 oz. soda.

When you have adjusted to the $1 per day, then try putting $2 per day in each category and adjusting the lifestyle again. When you have adapted to $2 then put $3 per day and so on until you are have the full 10% in each category every month and you lifestyle is maintained with 70% of your income. If you do this a little at a time, the lifestyle changes will seem minimal.

Of everything I have ever learned about money I feel this is the most important. The 70-10-10-10 rule. "They say" you only remember 10% of what you hear. If you don't remember anything from this book try to remember at least this chapter. It's the most important chapter of the book. If you never do anything financially other than discipline yourself to live the 70-10-10-10 rule you will be a master of money. Imagine the emotional freedom you will experience once you have mastered this strategy.

The brilliant part about the 70-10-10-10 strategy is it allows you to increase your lifestyle when you increase your earnings.

I have had several friends tell me they will maintain their current $50,000 lifestyle even when they are making $100,000. First of all BS, we always spend what we make. Second, why bother making more money if you're not going to use it to enhance your life? What's the point of giving up more minutes of your life to earn more money if you're not going to use it to better your life and the life of your family?

With the 70-10-10-10 strategy if you have a increase in pay you can increase the lifestyle just keep it at 70%. You can buy a bigger home, you can buy a nicer car, you can go out to fancy dinners as long as they all fit within the 70% category. If you were making $50,000 a year your lifestyle was 70% of $50,000 or $35,000 per year. Once you're making $100,000 your lifestyle is still 70% of the $100,000 but with a significant increase in the dollar amount to $70,000. You can use your money to enhance your lifestyle without feeling guilty. Don't be afraid of it, that's what it's for. Just make sure it stays in the 70-10-10-10 rule.

Don't get discouraged if this process doesn't go as fast as you would like it to. Once you get to the goal of 70-10-10-10 you will be more than able to make up for lost time. Congratulations, you are now a master of money.

One last question, what do you do with the money in the investing account?

The first dime you should ever spend out of your investing account should go towards your specialized financial education. Find someone who is an expert in the category you want to invest in and hire them to be your coach or mentor, buy their books, attend their seminars and don't forget all the free stuff like YouTube videos and podcasts and the endless information available at local public library. Learn everything you can before you spend one dime on the actual investment. If you don't spend it on your education you will pay for it one way or another don't try and fly your investment without instruction.

Don't worry if you can't come up with a financial investment right away. It may take you several months to find your first investment. Don't get discouraged just focus on the 70-10-10-10 rule and keep your eyes open for opportunities. The opportunity of a lifetime comes along once a week if you know what to look for. Soon you will be the one calling yourself lucky because you found the deal of a lifetime and no one else could see it.

Finding Startup Money

I walk into the back yard and open the door on the tool shed. The air conditioner on my car had stopped working for the third time that summer and I was looking for my toolbox. I moved my golf clubs to the side that were covered in dust and hadn't been used since I was flying private jets two years earlier. I then moved the snowboard that hadn't been used during the 4 years we were living in Florida. I hit my knee on some old pictures sitting on the floor that once had hung on the wall of our home years ago but were moved into storage when we repainted. We obviously hadn't missed them, I had forgotten they were there. I finally found the tool box and headed for the car to attempt the repairs on the air conditioning.

As I was laying in the dirt underneath the car trying to get the wrench into the small space that was obviously designed by an engineer and not a mechanic, my mind went back to all the stuff I had to move in the shed before I could get to my tools.

"Why in the world do we keep all that stuff?" I thought to myself. How ridiculous is it to keep all those things I don't even use? Why not sell them? My first thought was, *"well what if I need them?"* If I decide to go golfing again it would be nice to have them. Just then a second thought entered my mind that if turned into its physical equivalent would have felt like a kick in the butt.

"You haven't used that crap in years what makes you think your going to need it anytime soon?" I thought to myself.

If you sell the golf clubs and then decide to go golfing, rent or buy new ones, until then get rid of the stupid things. I dropped the wrench and headed for the shed. I started pulling out everything I had not used in years. Then I headed for the house. I went through everything that was taking up space and not being used. No more of this emotional attachment to stuff. Stuff that took up space in our small home and wasn't being used. It was yard sale time. Everything that wasn't currently being used was up for sale, coats, the clubs, the snowboard, even a few tools.

We made $1,000 in one day. We had a $1,000 worth of stuff just sitting around collecting dust and taking up space and getting in our way.

For weeks I had been complaining about not having money to afford paying a mechanic to fix the air conditioning on my car and now I had $1,000 in my pocket.

If you need a little start up cash, odds are you have it in your home already, it's time to clean house. Go through and find all the stuff you aren't using on a regular basis then sell it. No more emotional attachment to stuff. Use it or sell it, if you need it later, borrow it, rent it, or buy a new one but get rid of it for now. Turn it into cash then use the cash to buy an asset that makes you more money.

Summary

A green paper $100 bill sitting on a table is neither good nor evil. It by itself will never feed the hungry, nor will it turn itself into a handgun and harm a helpless animal. It can't make a man despise another man through a crooked business deal. It can't turn itself into a beautiful toy doll bringing a smile to a homeless child. It can't turn itself into a weapon of war killing thousands or turn itself into a powerful vaccine saving millions. No, the simply green piece of paper is just that, a piece of worthless paper. Good or evil exists only in the hearts of the human race.

The dollar is not greedy, generous, or emotional nor is it good nor evil, the human heart however is all of these things. The source of all good and evil is not money it's the human heart. Don't be fooled into believing otherwise.

Once you become a master of money it's up to you to do good or evil with your new fortune. Much like a handgun it can be used to protect you or destroy you. The money itself doesn't care who becomes a master of it, good or evil. Ethics and morals have nothing to do with one's ability to become rich. The love of money and the power it can bring has corrupted even the best of people and at the same time has saved countless lives through the charitable contributions of the good hearted. In the end the choice of what is being done with fortunes is decided by the person holding the money and what is in their heart.

When you become wealthy you will be criticized greatly by the less fortunate, relationships will change, friends will become enemies. Decide now who you want to be and stay in control of your emotions.

I have seen very wealthy people be criticized for not helping others. When in reality they have spent millions helping others anonymously. The big have big hearts and help on levels incomprehensible by the average 90 percenter.

The most valuable thing you could ever receive from the wealthy is information. The wealthy have taken what's most valuable to them -*time* - and spent it writing books, speaking at seminars, creating podcasts and all forms of social media just for you in an effort to free you from the prison created for your mind by the evil hearted.

Think about it, they are already wealthy, why waste the countless hours it takes to write a book or produce a podcast?

Once you discover true freedom and wealth you want to share it with the world. It's heartbreaking at the same time, only a small percentage will ever listen to what you have to say, but try you must.

The big have big hearts and want to help. Remember this the next time you are fortunate enough to speak face to face with a wealthy person, and remember Dabesir from

Babylon. He didn't ask the gold lender for money, he asked the gold lender to teach him how he made his gold.

Acknowledgments

First and foremost I would like to say thank you to my family most of all, to Cynthia for the editing and format and Breanna for the cover design. Trevor, Courtney and Jessica for your support and encouragement. I couldn't have done any of this without your help. You lived through it all with me and have been a tremendous help in creating, designing and the editing the book. I love you all and dedicate this book to you.

A special thanks to everyone of my friends and coworkers that helped with your input and feedback I truly am forever grateful.

To everyone who has read this book, I wish you success in your pursuit of true freedom and happiness.

Thank you with all of my heart.

Sincerely,
Todd Cook